MYSTERIES OF THE LORD'S PRAYER

MYSTERIES OF THE LORD'S PRAYER

Wisdom from the Early Church

John Gavin, SJ | Foreword by George Weigel

THE CATHOLIC UNIVERSITY OF AMERICA PRESS
Washington, D.C.

Library of Congress Cataloging-in-Publication Data
Names: Gavin, John, 1968– author. | Weigel, George, 1951– writer of foreword.
Title: The mysteries of the Lord's prayer : wisdom from the Early Church / John Gavin, SJ ;
foreword by George Weigel.
Description: Washington, D.C. : The Catholic University of America Press, [2021]
Identifiers: LCCN 2020056627 | ISBN 9780813233826 (paperback)
Subjects: LCSH: Lord's prayer. | Prayer—Christianity—History—Early church, ca. 30–600.
Classification: LCC BV230 .G38 2021 | DDC 226.9/6--dc23
LC record available at https://lccn.loc.gov/2020056627

To

Fr. Charles Dunn, SJ

Fr. John Gee

Fr. Paul McNellis, SJ

and

Fr. Ronald Tacelli, SJ

Four mentors in the priesthood and religious life

CONTENTS

ILLUSTRATIONS

George Weigel

In the middle decades of the twentieth century, while the Catholic Church in the United States was expanding its institutional infrastructure to meet the pastoral and educational needs of the children and grandchildren of nineteenth-century Catholic immigrants, Western European Catholicism was home to a Catholic theological renaissance that would have a profound effect on the world Church through the teaching of the Second Vatican Council.

That such a renaissance happened at all can seem implausible, even counterintuitive. For from the vantage point of the early twenty-first century, it certainly looks as if much of Europe was hell-bent on civilizational suicide in the years between the assassination of Archduke Franz Ferdinand and V-E Day—decades in which two extraordinarily bloody conflicts shredded the moral and cultural fabric of what had been, in 1914, the center of world civilization. Yet during and immediately after those cataclysms and partially in response to them, courageous European Catholic thinkers sought to renew Catholic theology and reenergize the Church's evangelical mission to a world that had lost its philosophical and moral bearings, with disastrous effects. They were primarily Francophones and native German-speakers, they knew classical languages, and their project would come to be known as *ressourcement*: the revitalization of Catholic theology and Catholic self-understanding through a "return to the sources" of Christian wisdom in Scripture and the Fathers of the Church.

That return was necessary because, in response to the intellectual assault on Catholicism mounted by the eighteenth- and nineteenth-century Continental Enlightenment, Catholic theology, often pushed in this direction by Rome, tended to withdraw into a defensive crouch. Thus to counter the claim of aggressive secularists and anticlerical politicians that thinkers like Voltaire, Comte, Feuerbach, Kant, Hume, Hegel, Darwin, Marx, and Nietzsche had effectively reduced Catholic doctrine to pious (or dangerous) myth, Catholic theologians deployed page after page of tightly reasoned syllogisms. Those exercises in logic had a certain solidity to them, and they could be persuasive within a certain frame of reference; but they had had little ability to win hearts or minds to Christ. More creative Catholic thinkers in the nineteenth century—Antonio Rosmini in Italy, Johann Adam Möhler and Matthias Scheeben in Germany, John Henry Newman in England—understood that this way of playing defense was bound to fail in a post-Kantian, post-Humean world insecure about its grasp on the truth of anything. So they tried, not without resistance from ecclesiastical authorities, to scout a path toward a more vibrant, less bone-dry form of Catholic theology, one that could introduce moderns to the person of Jesus Christ by communicating the perennial truths of the faith in an idiom that modern minds could engage. Their work would come to fruition in the twentieth century, after the trauma of two world wars had made unmistakably clear that, while a disenchanted world without God quickly turned into an abattoir, exercises in logic-chopping were insufficient in reconverting modernity and reconnecting Western civilization to one of its roots: biblical religion.

The birth of modern Catholic biblical studies under Pope

Leo XIII contributed much to this project of a "return to the sources," and the effects of a new Catholic biblical literacy can easily be seen in the central document of the Second Vatican Council, *Lumen Gentium* (The Dogmatic Constitution on the Church), which deployed dozens of biblical images to redescribe a Church that for some time had been content to style itself, rather coldly and juridically, as a *societas perfecta*: a "perfect society." Just as important to Vatican II's work, however, was the second dimension of mid-twentieth century Catholic theology's "return to the sources," which was the Catholic rediscovery and redeployment of the wisdom of the Fathers of the Church: the great theologian-pastors of the mid-centuries of the first millennium, who transformed the basic Christian kerygma—"Jesus is Lord"—into creed and doctrine, battling a host of heresies along the way. John Henry Newman, whose work on the Fathers eventually led him into full communion with the Catholic Church, was the nineteenth-century prophet of this patristic renaissance, which was then further developed by theologians like Romano Guardini, Henri de Lubac, Yves Congar, Joseph Ratzinger, and Hans Urs von Balthasar, whose imprint, like Newman's, can be found throughout Vatican II.

And at the center of this patristic renaissance, it could be argued, was a rediscovery of the Fathers' way of reading the Bible.

Unlike those defensive Catholic theologians of the nineteenth and early twentieth centuries who treated the Bible as a quarry from which to mine proof-texts, and unlike those modern "higher critics" who dissected the Bible as if it were a cadaver, the Fathers read Scripture as the living Word of God, in which God revealed himself and his salvific purposes, not merely ideas or propositions about himself. In other words, the Fathers read the Bible as a coherent whole in which one part illuminated other parts and the whole complex fit together as an endless source of insight into salvation history and its meaning for today.

Patristic biblical exegesis and commentary thus displayed an acute appreciation of what modern biblical scholar Raymond E. Brown called Scripture's *sensus plenior*, its "fuller sense"—which Father Brown defined in his doctoral dissertation as "that additional, deeper meaning, intended by God but not clearly intended by the human author, which is seen to exist in the words of a biblical text (or group of texts, or even a whole book) when they are studied in the light of further revelation or development in the understanding of revelation." And in doing all this, it might be noted, the patristic exegetes and commentators of the first Christian millennium were anticipating and practicing something similar to what late-twentieth- and twenty-first-century biblical scholars would call "canon criticism"—a holistic, rather than dissecting, approach to interpreting the books of the Bible and indeed to reading the Bible as a whole.

Father John Gavin's book on the Lord's Prayer is a welcome addition to this practice of reading Scripture through the eyes of the Fathers of the Church—saints and scholars whose wisdom is as vibrant and soul-nourishing today as it was a millennium and a half ago. The early North African Father Tertullian called the Lord's Prayer "the summary of the whole Gospel." By helping his readers understand and pray those familiar words with new insight drawn from ancient wisdom, Father Gavin reminds all of us that tradition, rightly understood, is not a dead letter; rather, tradition, whose Latin root means "handing on," is the living faith of those who have gone before us—and with whom we live, here and now, in the Communion of Saints. At the same time, Father Gavin reminds his fellow-theologians that a biblical exegesis that takes its only cues from contemporary academic fashions and fads drains theology of its capacity to be what its name implies—"speech about God"—and reduces it to another exercise in adolescent deconstruction.

The Christian proposal—which locates our humanity within

a great cosmic scheme of divine love revealing itself as the inner dynamic of all that is and will be—remains the most compelling summons to a genuine humanism on offer in the world today. At the heart of that proposal is the astonishing claim that we can address—we *must* address—that creating, redeeming, sanctifying love as "Father." The extraordinary quality of that claim can be lost by Christians whose been-there-done-that familiarity with the Lord's Prayer may have dulled their appreciation of its depths of meaning. By taking us into those depths with the help of St. Gregory of Nyssa, St. Cyril of Jerusalem, St. Peter Chrysologus, St. Cyprian, St. Augustine, and other Fathers of the Church, Father Gavin has enabled all who read this book to pray better— and to live more noble lives because of that prayer.

GEORGE WEIGEL is Distinguished Senior Fellow of Washington's Ethics and Public Policy Center, where he holds the William E. Simon Chair in Catholic Studies.

ACKNOWLEDGMENTS

One never reads the Scriptures and the Fathers alone. Thus, I am grateful to the community of scholars and students who have helped me in my reflection on the Lord's Prayer over the years. Versions of these chapters were given as papers in several forums: the Boston Colloquy in Historical Theology (Boston College, 2011); the Symposium on New Evangelization (Benedictine College, 2017); and the Canadian Society of Patristic Studies (Regina, SK, 2018). I am grateful for the feedback I received from the attending scholars and the ongoing conversations that have come from those encounters. Input from Prof. Khaled Anatolios, Fr. Paul Mankowski, SJ, and Prof. Susan Wessel proved extremely helpful in clarifying certain questions emerging from those presentations.

The College of the Holy Cross supported me during a semester leave (Spring 2019), during which I completed this volume. I am especially grateful to my chair, Fr. William Reiser, SJ, for encouraging me throughout the writing process.

I must also acknowledge one of my students, Claude Hanley, and the wonderful conversations we had during the composition of his senior thesis (2017–18) on Gregory of Nyssa's *De beatitudinibus*. Our talks helped me to become a better reader of Gregory.

The two anonymous readers of my manuscript provided outstanding comments and suggestions. This became a better book through their generous feedback.

This book would never have come to be without the encouragement and help of CUA Press editor John Martino. I cannot express sufficiently my gratitude for his guidance in this project.

My brother Pat, one of the smartest people I know, read and commented on early versions of this book. He saved me from serious gaffes and offered some wonderful suggestions. Any remaining errors are my own.

Finally, I would like to thank my parents, John and Patricia; my rector, Fr. Jim Stormes, SJ; and the Jesuit Community at the College of the Holy Cross for their prayers and support.

A. M. D. G.

INTRODUCTION

In this brief volume I offer a new way of reflecting on the Lord's Prayer that, in fact, is very old. This method comes from the Fathers of the Church, the ancient voices of sanctity and sagacity. These pages only provide a distillation of their wisdom.

The Fathers of the early centuries of Christianity include saints, scholars, bishops, priests, laity, and ascetics, who are all united in their hunger to know the Lord. Robert Louis Wilken writes that early Christian thinking "was as much an attempt to penetrate more deeply into the mystery of Christ, to know and understand what was believed and handed on in the churches, as it was to answer the charges of critics or explain the faith to outsiders."[1] Their writings that survive continue to inspire us in the pilgrimage toward the Father's house.

The Fathers found their font of wisdom in the Scriptures: they were, first and foremost, disciples of the Word. The manner in which they read the Bible as the living Word of God therefore demands our attention. Though they understood there to be a literal meaning in the Scriptures, they also sought the deeper, spiritual meanings beneath the often-confusing verses. Their explication of the Scriptures was an act of prayer that called upon the Holy Spirit for guidance. In the light of Christ, the Bible was a mystery that revealed itself in the humble reading of the Church.

1. Robert Louis Wilken, *The Spirit of Early Christian Thought: Seeking the Face of God* (New Haven: Yale University Press, 2003), 3.

Thus, we could ask for no better teachers in a careful and prayerful examination of the Lord's Prayer. Cyprian, Origen, Augustine, Jerome, Maximus, and others will reveal to us not only the puzzling nature of Christ's words, but also their transformative power. Christ told his disciples to "pray like this," to make the prayer a model for their lives. The Fathers will help us to understand just what Jesus' command means.

Note on translations: Unless otherwise noted, English translations of texts are my own. Biblical translations, unless otherwise noted, are from the Revised Standard Version.

ABBREVIATIONS

Abbreviations for Series

CCG	Corpus Christianorum Series Graeca
CCL	Corpus Christianorum Series Latina
CSEL	Corpus Scriptorum Ecclesiasticorum Latinorum
GNO	Gregorii Nysseni Opera
LCL	Loeb Classical Library
PG	Patrologia Graeca
PL	Patrologia Latina
PTS	Patristische Texte und Studien
SC	Sources Chrétiennes

Abbreviations for Commonly Cited Texts

Beat.	Gregory of Nyssa, *De beatitudinibus* ["On the Beatitudes"]
Catecheses	Cyril of Jerusalem, *Catecheses mystagogicae quinque* ["Mystagogical Catechesis"]
Col. serm.	Peter Chrysologus, *Collectio sermonum* ["Sermons"]
Col.	John Cassian, *Collationes* ["Conferences"]
De oratione	Tertullian, *De oratione* ["On Prayer"]

De oratione dom.	Cyprian of Carthage, *De oratione dominica* ["On the Lord's Prayer"]
De or.	Origen of Alexandria, *De oratione* ["On Prayer"]
De or. dom.	Gregory of Nyssa, *De oratione dominica* ["On the Lord's Prayer"}
De serm. Dom.	Augustine of Hippo, *De sermone Domini in monte* ["On the Lord's Sermon on the Mount"]
In Matthaeum	John Chrysostom, *Homiliae in Matthaeum* (F. Field edition) ["Homilies on Matthew"]
In Matt.	Jerome of Stridon, *In Mattheum* ["On Matthew"]
Or. dom.	Maximus the Confessor, *Expositio orationis dominicae* ["Commentary on the Lord's Prayer"]
Regula	*Regula magistri* ["Rule of the Master"]
Serm.	Augustine of Hippo, *Sermones* ["Sermons"]

MYSTERIES OF THE LORD'S PRAYER

1

ENTERING THE MYSTERIES

The Earliest Commentary on the Lord's Prayer?

The city of Pompeii succumbed to the wrath of Mount Vesuvius on August 24, 79 A.D. Pliny the Younger offered an eyewitness account of the volcano's power as it obliterated the city and took the life of his uncle, Pliny the Elder:

You could hear the shrieks of women, the wailing of infants, and the shouting of men; some were calling their parents, others their children or their wives, trying to recognize them by their voices. People bewailed their own fate or that of their relatives, and there were some who prayed for death in their terror of dying. Many besought the aid of the gods, but still more imagined there were no gods left, and that the universe was plunged into eternal darkness for evermore.[1]

The moving evidence of Pompeii's tragedy that remains to this day includes bodies eerily preserved beneath the ash. These ruins may give testimony to the death of the gods, but one archeological discovery amidst the carnage may point toward the advent of a new faith. It is a puzzle in more than one sense and a curiosity that demonstrates both remarkable linguistic ingenuity and,

1. Pliny the Younger, *Letters: Books 1–7*, ed., trans. Betty Radice, LCL 55 (Cambridge, Mass.: Harvard University Press, 1969), 444–45.

perhaps, the fruit of spiritual reflection. In a city of death, this artifact, the ROTAS-SATOR square, remains a living enigma.

The ROTAS-SATOR square is a two-dimensional palindrome —it can be read backward and forward in two directions—that has been found in other sites up through the Middle Ages, but the example found etched in Pompeii stands out as the oldest, given that it must date before the eruption in 79 A.D. One does not need to know Latin in order to appreciate the genius of its author (see figure 1-1).

Figure 1-1. ROTAS-SATOR Square

R	O	T	A	S
O	P	E	R	A
T	E	N	E	T
A	R	E	P	O
S	A	T	O	R

Four of the words in this two-dimensional palindrome are easily recognizable Latin: *rotas* (accusative plural, "wheels"), *opera* (accusative plural, "works"), *tenet* ("he/she has, holds") and *sator* (nominative singular, "sower, farmer"). *Arepo* cannot be found in a Latin dictionary, and some scholars consider it to be a name. As for the meaning of the sentence, one can find no solid consensus. Perhaps one could render it, "The farmer Arepo has wheels as his works"—that is, "The farmer Arepo has a plow for his work." Yet, it may also be a nonsense phrase produced by the palindromic structure. Its pleasure and, for many, its mystical power belong to the astonishing production of a sentence that never closes, no matter which way one turns.

But there is more. In addition to being a palindrome, the square may also be cast as both an anagram and a pictogram. A rearrangement of the letters produces figure 1-2. The square transforms into a cruciform *Pater Noster*, or "Our Father," with the remaining letters repeating *A* and *O*, Latin substitutes for *A* and Ω, the first and last letters of the Greek alphabet.[2]

Figure 1-2. ROTAS-SATOR Anagram

					P				
					A				
					T				
A					E			O	
					R				
P	A	T	E	R	N	O	S	T	E	R
					O				
A					S			O	
					T				
					E				
					R				

Could this remarkable square be, in fact, the earliest Christian, nonscriptural commentary on the Lord's Prayer? Numerous problems militate against giving it a Christian provenance;[3] yet

2. On the astronomical odds of the square randomly producing such an anagram, see Duncan Fishwick, "On the Origin of the Rotas-Sator Square," *Harvard Theological Review* 57, no. 1 (1964): 42.

3. For example, it is difficult for many scholars to believe that there were already Latin-speaking Christians in Pompeii by 79 A.D. Furthermore, the *A* and Ω seem to be a reference to Rv 22:13, to which most scholars assign a later date. Yet some make the case for a Christian provenance. For a summary and theories, see Hugh Last, "The Rotas-Sator Square: Present Positions and Future Prospects," *Journal of Theological Studies* 3, no. 1 (1952): 95–97. On a possible Jewish origin, see Nicolas Vinel,

Christians of later centuries most certainly adopted it as their own, even etching it into churches.[4] I shall return to the fruits of this illuminating commentary later in this chapter, but first a review of the Lord's Prayer, the focus of this book, is in order.

Which Version Is the Real Lord's Prayer?

Christians throughout the world recite the Lord's Prayer on a daily basis in private devotions, the liturgy, the rosary, and many other occasions. It is truly the universal prayer that unites all followers of Christ. They inherently recognize that the recitation of Jesus' own words inserts them into a radical relationship with the Creator God. In this prayer the Lord calls them "to share—through the supernatural gift of grace—in his intimate life, his possessions, his beatitude, in the heritage of his incomprehensible and infinitely transcendent Godhead."[5]

Yet many Christians fail to recognize that the version they regularly recite may differ significantly from the authoritative versions that come down to us. The Scriptures, in fact, contain two different forms of the prayer, while a significant first-century witness, the *Didache* (*The Teaching of the Twelve Apostles*), has a version that differs slightly from those of the gospels. Brief examinations of fresh translations reveal some important features that will become significant in subsequent chapters (see figure 1-3).

"Le judaïsme caché du carré Sator de Pompéi," *Revue de l'histoire des religions* 223, no. 2 (2006): 173–94; Roy Hammerling, *The Lord's Prayer in the Early Church: The Pearl of Great Price* (New York: Palgrave Macmillan, 2010), 22–25.

4. For a recent discovery of a square etched onto a church wall in the sixteenth century, see Christopher Howse, "Unique Ancient Sator-Rotas Word-Square Discovered," *Telegraph*, May 2, 2015, http://www.telegraph.co.uk/comment/11579586/Unique-ancient-Sator-Rotas-word-square-discovered.html.

5. Raïssa Maritain, *Notes on the Lord's Prayer*, ed. Jacques Maritain (New York: P. J. Kennedy and Sons, 1963), 20.

Figure 1-3. Versions of the Lord's Prayer

Mt 6:9–13	Lk 11:2–4	*Didache*
Our Father who are in the heavens, let your name be hallowed. Let your kingdom come. Let your will be done, on earth as in heaven. Give us today our daily/future/super-substantial bread. And forgive us our debts, as we too have forgiven our debtors. And do not lead us into temptation/trial, but rescue us from Evil/the Evil One.	Father, let your name be hallowed. Let your kingdom come. Give us daily our daily/future/super-substantial bread. And forgive us our sins, for we ourselves also forgive each one who is in debt to us.	Our Father who are in heaven, let your name be hallowed. Let your kingdom come. Let your will be done, on earth as in heaven. Give us today our daily/future/super-substantial bread. And forgive us our debt, as we too forgive our debtors. And do not lead us into temptation/trial, But rescue us from Evil/the Evil one. Because yours is the power and the glory forever.

Note: For the Greek text of the *Didache*, see *The Didache: Faith, Hope, and Life of the Earliest Christian Communities 50–70 C.E.,* ed. Aaron Milavec (New York: Newman Press, 2003), 30.

The gospels clearly hold the greatest authority for the transmission of Jesus' prayer. Yet, how can one reconcile their strikingly different versions? Why does Matthew have "Our Father" and Luke have only "Father"? Why doesn't Luke include the petition regarding the Father's will? What happened to the conclusion of the prayer in Luke's version? Why does Matthew speak only of debts and debtors, while Luke of sins and debtors?

The third-century theologian Origen of Alexandria stands out as one Father who sought to explain the discrepancies. As a close reader of the Scriptures, he notes the distinct contexts in which Jesus teaches the prayer: in the Gospel of Matthew, Jesus gives this model prayer within the collection of teachings known as the Sermon on the Mount, a "private" address to a select audience; in the Gospel of Luke, it is found in a public response to a disciple's desire to pray as Jesus prays. According to Origen, Jesus therefore deliberately taught two different versions of the prayer according to the needs of particular audiences. Yet, this does not mean that the prayers diverge in their essential meanings. "But perhaps it might be suggested that the prayers are equivalent in meaning, and are to be discussed as though they were one, once as in a private communication [Matthew's Sermon on the Mount] and then at the request of another of the disciples [Luke's version], who surely was not present when Jesus spoke what is recorded by Matthew, unless he had forgotten what had been spoken earlier."[6] Origen therefore resolves the discrepancies by making the Lucan version a brief summary of the Matthean version that Jesus gives to an absent, or perhaps absentminded, follower.

Modern biblical scholars do not follow Origen's solution, though they generally agree with the Alexandrian regarding distinct *audiences*. Each gospel writer adapted a Greek translation of a prayer originally said in Aramaic, attempting to compensate for linguistic and cultural gaps in two different audiences through their selection of words and the overall structure. On the one hand, Luke's prayer, written for a Gentile audience, represents the original structure and length of the Aramaic, while Matthew's offers a more developed version of the prayer for liturgical use in a Jewish-Christian community. On the other hand, Matthew seems to have preserved a wording closer to the Aramaic, while Luke adapted the vocabulary for his non-Jewish audience.[7]

---

6. Origen of Alexandria, *De oratione*, PG 11, 473D, in *On the Lord's Prayer: Tertullian, Cyprian and Origen on the Lord's Prayer*, trans. Alistair Stewart-Sykes (Crestwood, N.Y.: St. Vladimir's Seminary Press, 2004), 154. For an overview of the versions of the prayer in Matthew and Luke, see C. Clifton Black, *The Lord's Prayer* (Louisville: Westminster John Knox Press, 2018), 43–48.

7. For instance, Luke uses "forgive us our *sins*" instead of "forgive us our *debts*" because his Gentile audience would not have immediately understood the Jewish

The *Didache* provides catechetical instruction, as well as teachings regarding rituals and Church organization. Its version of the prayer hews closely to that of Matthew, though one can quickly discover some slight variations—for instance, "heaven" instead of "heavens"; "debt" instead of "debts." In particular, the work adds a doxology—a proclamation of God's glory—at the conclusion, followed by the instruction to offer the Lord's Prayer three times a day. It most likely emerges from the liturgical context of the early Christian community.

So, which is the "real" prayer that Jesus gave his disciples? Attempts to reconstruct the original Aramaic can be illuminating, but in the end, they are only educated speculations. The Fathers of the Church and most Christian liturgies opt for some adaptation of the Matthean prayer, since it provides an ampler series of points for reflection. Yet this predilection for Matthew should not lead one to discount the succinct rendition of Luke, since he does provide some enlightening commentary through his choices in words, tenses, and structure. In the end, it is best to follow Origen's advice and see them as a single prayer: Matthew and Luke give us complementary insights into Jesus' teachings, while the *Didache* opens a window onto the living practice of the prayer among the earliest Christians.

Why Reflect on the Lord's Prayer?

Why does the Church return again and again to the Lord's Prayer? Jesus, in giving this prayer, told his disciples "to pray in this way" or "to pray like this" (Mt 6:9)—that is, it is the truest model of all Christian prayer. The early Church recognized the

---

metaphor of "debt" for "sin." For a general overview of these positions, see W. F. Albright and C. S. Mann, *Matthew: Introduction, Translation, and Notes* (New York: Doubleday, 1971), 75–77; Joseph Fitzmyer, *The Gospel According to Luke X–XXIV* (New York: Paulist Press, 1985), 896–97; Joachim Jeremias, *The Prayers of Jesus*, trans. John Reumann (Philadelphia: Fortress, 1978), 93.

sacredness of these verses and made them part of its liturgical life early on, even reserving the prayer to the baptized faithful.[8] The second/third-century theologian Tertullian wrote that the Lord's Prayer is "a summary of the whole Gospel."[9] A reflection on the prayer therefore brings us to the heart of Jesus' teaching and to the source of the Church's spirituality. Today the Church desperately needs to rediscover the meaning and power of calling God "Our Father" in a broken world. Romano Guardini gave this advice some decades ago: "And at a time when we feel so many things shaken to their foundations, we have every reason to grope our way back to the very core of the Christian realities wherein the undisturbed omnipotence of the Redemption reigns."[10]

The ROTAS-SATOR square, presented at the beginning of this chapter, provides further justifications. First, the *Pater Noster* that comes from the square appears in the form of a cross. Since the prayer is "a summary of the whole Gospel," this should not be surprising. The prayer takes its structure from the very mission of the Son, the journey from his self-emptying affirmation of the Father's will to his triumphant death upon the cross. Though, as we shall see, the prayer was *not* the model for Jesus' own prayer, it nonetheless takes its form from Christ's descent—the incarnation of the Son—and ascent—his ascension to the Father—in his mission to restore all things to the Father. The cross—the sign of ignominy that became the symbol of redemption—embraces the world from four directions with the power of the Incarnate Word's self-gift. The Lord's Prayer therefore rightfully assumes

---

8. See Willy Rordorf, "The Lord's Prayer in the Light of Its Liturgical Use in the Early Church," *Studia Liturgica* 14 (1980–81): 3; Raymond Brown, "The *Pater Noster* as an Eschatological Prayer," in *New Testament Essays* (New York: Paulist Press, 1968), 177–78; G. W. Lampe, "'Our Father' in the Fathers," in *Christian Spirituality: Essays in Honor of Gordon Rupp*, ed. Peter Brooks (London: S. C. M. Press, 1975), 11.

9. Tertullian, *Breviarium totius Evangelii*; *De oratione* 1, PL 1, 1153B.

10. Romano Guardini, *The Lord's Prayer*, trans. Isabel McHugh (New York: Pantheon, 1958), 8.

the cruciform to embrace the Church and transform the life of the believer.

The one who prays the Lord's Prayer therefore agrees to follow the Way of the Cross established by Christ. The prayer provides a map for body and spirit; it guides both the individual and the community through the appropriation of the Christ's descent and ascent. Jesus gave this prayer to us because to recite it and to live it conforms us to himself, the Lord who triumphed upon the cross.

Next, the ROTAS-SATOR commentary inserts the prayer within the double Alpha and Omega, implying that we must reflect upon the prayer in two different ways: as the Beginning and as the End. First, the two letters refer to Christ's exhilarating promise and strong warning from the book of Revelation: "Behold, I am coming soon, bringing my recompense, to repay every one for what he has done. I am the *Alpha* and the *Omega*, the first and the last, the beginning and the end" (Rv 22:12–13). The prayer must therefore be understood within a vision of the coming fulfillment of creation in Christ—a vision that demands a radical reorientation of our lives.

The Scripture scholar Raymond Brown considered the *Pater Noster* to be an eschatological prayer. He defined "eschatological" as "the period of last days, involving the return of Christ, the destruction of the forces of evil and the definite establishment of God's rule."[11] The audacious proclamation of God as "Father," as well as the hope for the unification of heaven and earth under his rule and will, indicate a change in the relationship between humanity and God that has yet to come to full fruition. In turn, all the petitions express a yearning for a new order in which trust in God ("give us our daily bread"), reconciliation ("forgive us our debts"), and liberation from Evil ("rescue us from the Evil One") will re-form creation. The prayer therefore should awaken

11. Raymond Brown, "*Pater Noster*," 175.

Christians who have become too content with the affairs of the world. It reorients their desires and hopes. Their fulfillment lies outside of their power, and an unexpected, glorious end has yet to come.[12]

A reflection on the Lord's Prayer should therefore give us a supernatural outlook. This does not mean that the prayer does not have immediate ethical and social implications. The Christian lives in the world and has received the mission to transform it from within. Yet the prayer should also topple our personal domiciles built on the sands of worldly complacency and transfer our hearts to the mansion of the Father, to the house built on the rock of Christ. If the itinerary of the prayer is the Way of the Cross, then the Christian must see all things within the liberating power of the Word Made Flesh. The concluding "deliver us" implies not only escape, but also a completion that can only come from God. Our eyes must look toward Christ, who is not only the Beginning of all things, but also the End for whom all things yearn.

Second, the prayer demands that each person replace incarcerating solipsism with divine liberation. In the twenty-first century, in particular, each person tends to see himself as his own Beginning and End. We define not only *who* we are, but also *what* we are. We *begin* from the exercise of our freedom—a freedom indifferent to human nature and virtue—and *end* in the assertion of disparate, competing selves upon the world. Our ever-growing scientific control over physical birth and death has deluded us into thinking that we now control these intimate mysteries. We have become a legion of narcissistic angels—what we once called demons—since each one defines his own identity or species. Because each Beginning and End is contained within the self, our

12. "Nevertheless, as we say the prayer nineteen centuries later, now completely enmeshed in the temporal aspect of the Christian life, it would, perhaps, profit us to revive in part some of its original eschatological yearning"; Raymond Brown, "*Pater Noster*," 202.

society—including many Christians—consists of millions of incarcerated persons.

A reflection upon the Lord's Prayer replaces our selfish Beginning and End with the Alpha and Omega of Christ. We escape the prison of solipsism through the liberating life of the Incarnate Word. The mystic Adrienne von Speyr wrote of this new freedom: "This is the true gift that the Lord brings to us when he lives our temporal life and lives out that life from his eternity: he will also be, through this living, the Beginning and the End in us, after he has shared with us this Alpha-and-Omega-*Being* through his Beginning-and-Ending-*having* in our temporal existence."[13] In becoming man, the Son liberates us from sin by *having* our humanity united to himself and thereby bringing us into his divine *Being*: the Son *has* our human existence in the incarnation that we might *be* in his divine life. "The Word of God, our Lord Jesus Christ, who did, through His transcendent love, become what we are, that He might bring us to be even what He is Himself."[14] Jesus mediates between time and eternity, taking on what we have and sharing what he has—that is, his very self, from Beginning to End. The Lord's Prayer recreates by giving us our true Alpha and Omega.

The book of Revelation summarizes what I have presented here in a much clearer and dramatic way:

The one who sat on the throne [God the Father] said, "Behold, I make all things new." Then he said, "Write these words down, for they are trustworthy and true." He said to me, "They are accomplished. I am the Alpha and the Omega, the Beginning and the End. To the thirsty I will give a gift from the spring of life-giving water. The victor will inherit these gifts, and I shall be his God, and he will be my son. But as for cowards, the unfaithful, the depraved, murderers, the unchaste,

13. Adrienne von Speyr, *Apokalypse: Betrachtungen über die Geheime Offenbarung* (Vienna: Verlag Herold, 1950), 808.

14. Irenaeus of Lyon, *Contra haereses* V [*Contre les Hérésies* V], ed. Adelin Rousseau, SC 153 (Paris: Éditions Cerf, 1969), 14, lines 36–39.

sorcerers, idol-worshipers, and deceivers of every sort, their lot is in the burning pool of fire and sulfur, which is the second death." (Rv 21:5–8)

In this passage God the Father proclaims a new order. Since the Father and Son are one in their divinity, both are the Beginning and the End of all things.[15] Those who escape solipsism and share in the life of Christ as their Beginning and End may therefore boldly call God *Father*: "I shall be his God, and he will be my son." But to those who enclose themselves within a self-designed Beginning and End, there is only a "second death." The ROTAS-SATOR square, in placing the Lord's Prayer between the Alpha and the Omega, tells us that the prayer itself will recreate us from Beginning to End.

How to Proceed?

There are many ways to enter the mysteries of the Lord's Prayer. In recent years scholars have paid particular attention to such issues as its structure, its relationship to Jewish prayers, and its place within the overall context of the Scriptures. Their studies have cleared away many of the preconceptions that have prevented us from perceiving the marvels of Jesus' teachings in these brief words.[16] I certainly intend to avail myself of the fruits of these tremendous labors in this series of reflections.

15. "Can there be two *Alphas*, two beginnings? How can both the Father and Christ be *Alpha* and *Omega*? Here is further proof of the co-equality and consubstantiality of the Father and the Son. Both God the Father and Christ the Son are *Alpha* and *Omega*, for Christ is one with His Father" (Jn 10:30); Lawrence Farley, *The Apocalypse of St. John: A Revelation of Love and Power* (Chesterton, Ind.: Conciliar Press, 2011), 225. Also see Peter Williamson, *Revelation* (Grand Rapids, Mich.: Baker Academic, 2015), 365.

16. John Dominic Crossan begins his book on the Lord's Prayer with a prologue entitled, "The Strangest Prayer." He notes, "It is prayed in all churches, but it never mentions church. It is prayed on all Sundays, but it never mentions Sunday. It is called the 'Lord's Prayer,' but it never mentions 'Lord.' Indeed, this prayer needs to become strange to us again in order to reshape our spiritual lives"; Crossan, *The*

Yet this still leaves the question of how to find a gateway and a path. We could, perhaps, allow the structure of the prayer to guide us. Take, for example, two classical works by the German-Italian theologian Romano Guardini and the French philosopher and mystic Raïssa Maritain. Romano Guardini, in his profound reflections upon the prayer, followed the classic division of seven petitions (see "Thou [Your] Petitions" and "We [Us] Petitions" at the end of this paragraph). Yet, he surprisingly began with "Thy Will be Done" as the gateway into the prayer: all the petitions help us to conform to the transformative divine will. Raïssa Maritain, the philosopher and mystic, also followed the petitionary itinerary; however, she highlighted two categories of the petitions: the first three "thou" petitions turn us toward God,[17] while the remaining four "we" petitions express our supplications before the loving Creator. Despite the differences, the reflections of both these authors result from a widely acknowledged structure:

Thou [Your] Petitions
1. Our Father who are in the heavens
2. Let your name be hallowed
3. Let your kingdom come

We [Us] Petitions
1. Give us this day our daily bread
2. And forgive us our debts, as we also forgive our debtors
3. And lead us not into temptation
4. But rescue us from Evil [the Evil One]

Greatest Prayer: *Rediscovering the Revolutionary Message of the "The Lord's Prayer"* (New York: HarperCollins, 2010), 1.

17. Like Guardini, Raïssa Maritain sees the conformity to Christ as the key to the personal and ecclesial appropriation of the prayer. "This prayer begins in a turning toward God and the goodness of God. In the first three petitions Christ unites us to himself in solemn and admirable supplications, Jesus' desires and our own, addressed to the common Father"; Maritain, *Notes on the Lord's Prayer*, 23.

This volume, while acknowledging the fruit of these approaches, will follow a different path: the way of *aporiai*—that is, "problems" or "obstacles."[18] Problems in the scriptural text inspire modern students to dig deeply into the sources of history, the fonts of philology, and the resources of interpretive schools. However, for the Fathers of the Church, who will serve as our primary guides in these reflections, puzzling passages acted as flags or signs of hidden springs waiting to burst forth. The third-century theologian Origen of Alexandria noted the necessity and challenge of problem solving for the reverent reader of God's Word:

> One must by all means be persuaded, once one has accepted that these Scriptures are the work of the world's Creator, that those who investigate the Scriptures will confront issues as serious as do those who investigate the rational principles of creation. Indeed, even in creation there exist some problems which human nature finds it hard or impossible to resolve, but the Creator of the Universe is not to be blamed on this account; for example, we do not ascertain the cause of the creation of basilisks or other venomous beasts. In the case of someone who perceives the weakness of our race and that it is impossible for us to comprehend the rational principles of God's skill even when they have been contemplated with very precise attention, the reverent procedure is to refer the knowledge of these which we piously pay attention may be revealed to us. Similarly, in the divine Scriptures one must see that there are many problems hard for us to resolve.[19]

---

18. The way of *aporiai* antedates Christianity. For instance, the Platonic dialogues often posed *aporiai* as philosophical dilemmas that inspire one to confront significant metaphysical problems and to trace the problems to their source. For the use of "aporetic inquiry" by Plato, see the commentary in Plato, *Plato's "Parmenides": Translation and Analysis*, trans. R. E. Allen (Minneapolis: University of Minnesota Press, 1983), 96–98, 180.

19. Origen of Alexandria, *Commentary on Psalm 5* [*Philocalie, 1–20: Sur les Écritures*], ed. Marguerite Harl, SC 302 (Paris: Éditions Cerf, 1983), 246–48, lines 1–15, in Joseph W. Trigg, *Origen* (New York: Routledge, 1998), 71–72.

Problems, or *aporiai*, in the Scriptures should therefore engage the reader as clear invitations from God. Yet, at the same time, the reader should always tackle them with great reverence and humility. *Aporiai* may not have a single answer, since the questions they pose only give limited and formative glimpses into the infinite divine mystery.[20] In fact, one could say that scriptural *aporiai* deliberately keep us humble and force us to adopt the truest approach to God: contemplation and an abandonment to the Spirit. When we hang our heads in exhaustion before a difficulty we have vainly attempted to master, we can only turn to God and ask that it "may be revealed to us."

Through a reading of the Fathers we can discover a series of *aporiai* that engaged them in their reading of the Lord's Prayer. Some of these puzzles continue to stimulate contemporary scholarship; others leave modern scholars smiling and shaking their heads. I have selected the most prominent problems in the hope that the reflections will bring the greatest fruit to the reader. In the end, this volume will not offer definitive answers to the questions, but rather, thanks to the wisdom of the Fathers, it hopes to provide inspiring responses that will guide one on the Way of the Cross to the One who is our Beginning and End.

20. "The Church Fathers, however, took it as self-evident that the words of the Bible often had multiple meanings and the plain sense did not exhaust their meaning"; Wilken, *Spirit of Early Christian Thought*, 70.

2

FIRST *APORIA*

HOW CAN HUMAN BEINGS CALL GOD
"FATHER"?

Confronting a Bold Claim

Though familiarity may not always breed contempt, it very often leads to indifference. Christians have been addressing the Creator as "Father" for so long that the strangeness of this form of address no longer scandalizes them. Instead, they proclaim God to be their Father as if to do so were their birthright.

Furthermore, today the word "Father" inspires a host of connotations and feelings: familiarity and authority; security and fear; respect and resentment. Fatherhood impresses every person on account of the varying quality of its presence or the wounds stemming from its absence. Thus, one can ask: Is it appropriate to apply such a loaded word to the transcendent God? Christ may have effectively mandated its use, but how can we humans use it without infecting it with our own experiences and prejudices? Claiming filial kinship with the Creator should disturb every person who pronounces the words of the Lord's Prayer.

The Fathers generally treated two issues within this *aporia*:

divine unknowability and human sinfulness. These problems challenged the Fathers of the Church in their attempts to resolve the question before them: how can mere human beings call God "Father"?

Divine Unknowability

Christians affirm that God does not belong to the created order. God is not a demiurge—a super-being who organized preexisting material to create the cosmos—and human categories cannot define him. Thus, God's transcendence makes him unknowable in his essence. Reflection upon the created order may allow humans to know *that* God is, but they can never know *what* God is. The giant of Latin-speaking Christianity, Augustine of Hippo, once preached, "If it is God that you grasped, it is not God; if you were able to understand, you understood something else in place of God."[1] And the fourth-century bishop Gregory of Nyssa brings this point home: "The Divine Nature, whatever it may be in itself, surpasses every mental concept. For it is altogether inaccessible to reasoning and conjecture, nor has there been found any human faculty capable of perceiving the incomprehensible; for we cannot devise a means of understanding inconceivable things."[2]

Given that humans cannot put God into a categorical box without rendering him another object in the created world, how

---

1. "Si cepisti, non est Deus; si comprehendere potuisti, aliud pro Deo comprehendisti"; Augustine of Hippo, *Serm.* 52, PL 38, 360.

2. Gregory of Nyssa, *De beatitudinibus* 6, ed. J. Callahan, GNO 7. 2 (New York: Brill, 1992), 140, lines 15–20, in *The Lord's Prayer and the Beatitudes*, trans. Hilda Graef (New York: Paulist Press, 1954), 146. The believer, writes Henri de Lubac, has a general sense of this divine unknowability. "Our concepts have the power to *signify* God truly—and yet strictly speaking, we cannot *seize* God in any one of them; or rather that is how they truly signify him. God would not be God unless he were—not unknowable but—beyond our grasp. He is always above and beyond all that we can say and think of him"; de Lubac, SJ, *The Discovery of God*, trans. Alexander Dru (Grand Rapids, Mich.: Eerdmans, 1996), 128–29.

can they call him "Father"?[3] Doesn't a name make him comprehensible? Even the excuse that the title "Father" comes from revealed language in the Scriptures—from the Savior himself—does not resolve this issue. As we have already seen, the word "Father" is a loaded term, replete with the baggage of human experience. It drives us into the illusion that we *know* God as another figure in our familial ambit; it encourages an intimacy that audaciously, and perhaps deleteriously, transgresses the insurmountable divide between creature and Creator.

In fact, the Fathers regularly stress that Christians must avoid anthropomorphisms—human qualities applied to nonhuman objects—when speaking of the divine. The temptation to depict God as a superhuman not only shackles God within the chains of created contingency, but can also contribute to human pride: God is one of *us*, only on a larger scale. In fact, the tradition of the *via negativa*—we do better to state what God is not than what God is—has long provided a sobering safeguard against such human hubris.[4] Calling God Father, therefore, implies a dangerous attempt to transform God into an object for human analysis and control.

3. One *aporia* that will not be addressed in this book is, "Is the Father the name for the Father of the Son or for the Trinity?" For instance, Augustine, in his *De Trinitate*, allows for one application of the name "Father" metaphorically to the entire Trinity, since the Trinity effects our divine adoption as sons and daughters. Yet, as we shall see, Maximus the Confessor clearly identifies "Father" with the Father of the Son. See Augustine of Hippo, *The Trinity* V.3.12, trans. Edmund Hill, OP (New York: New City Press, 1991), 198–99.

4. The mysterious figure who called himself Dionysius the Areopagite stressed the dangers of overreaching the limitations of human expression. One cannot grasp the Divinity that is beyond all essences. See Pseudo-Dionysius the Areopagite, *De divinis nominibus* 1.5, ed. B. R. Suchla, PTS 33 (Berlin: De Gruyter, 1990), 116, in *Pseudo-Dionysius: The Complete Works*, trans. Colm Luibheid (New York: Paulist Press, 1987), 54–55.

Human Sinfulness

The Fathers faced the problem of human sinfulness. How can we—sinners, one and all—dare to claim filial rights from the All-Holy One? Gregory of Nyssa summarizes the problem well:

Supposing a man should try to understand God as far as possible from the names that have been invented for Him and so be led to the understanding of the ineffable glory; he would have learned that the Divine Nature, whatever it may be in itself, is absolute goodness, holiness and joy, power, glory and purity, eternity that is always absolutely the same. These and whatever other things thought could learn about the Divine Nature, whether from the Divine Scriptures or from its own mediation, he would consider—and after all that should he dare to utter such a word and call this Being his Father? If he has any sense, he would obviously not dare to call God by the name Father since he does not see the same things in himself as he sees in God. For it is physically impossible that He who is good by essence should be the Father of an evil will.[5]

The old adage "Like Father, like son" serves as the foundation for this problem: If we human beings claim to be sons and daughters of God, we are also claiming that God is like we are. Yet, since we are sinners, we are effectively claiming that *God too is sinful*. This, of course, would be blasphemy. Human beings, therefore, should not dare to call God "our Father."

Responding to the Problems

In their commentaries on the Lord's Prayer, the Fathers respond to these challenges through reflection upon two major themes: divine adoption and growth in the divine likeness.

---

5. Gregory of Nyssa, *De oratione dominica* 2, ed. J. Callahan, GNO 7.2 (New York: Brill, 1992), 23, lines 11–25, in Graef, *Lord's Prayer and the Beatitudes*, 38.

Divine Adoption

The Fathers acquire the theme of adoption from their reading of the Scriptures. St. Paul, in the Letter to the Galatians, wrote that "God sent forth his Son, born of a woman, born under the law, to redeem those under the law so that we might receive adoption as sons" (4:4–5). The Letter to the Ephesians beautifully portrays this new filial relationship between God and humanity as the very foundation of creation:

> He destined us in love to be his sons through Jesus Christ, according to the purpose of his will, to the praise of his glorious grace which he freely bestowed on us in the Beloved.... For he has made known to us in all wisdom and insight the mystery of his will, according to his purpose which he set forth in Christ as a plan for the fullness of time, to unite all things in him, things in heaven and things on earth. (Eph 1: 5–6; 9–10)

The Gospel of John makes it clear that this adoption takes place through Jesus: "But to all who received him, who believed in his name, he gave power to become children of God; who were born, not of blood nor of the will of the flesh nor of the will of man, but of God" (Jn 1:12–13). Therefore, Jesus himself brings his disciples into the intimacy of this life. Through him they will come to abide in his Father's house as members of his family: "In my Father's house are many rooms; if it were not so, would I have told you that I go to prepare a place for you?" (Jn 14:2).

The Gospel of Matthew also makes this point through Jesus' use of the expressions "my Father/the Father" (twenty-six citations), "your Father" (eighteen citations), and "our Father" (one citation, found only in Matthew's Gospel in the Lord's Prayer). Jesus uses "my Father" to indicate his unique relationship: he alone possesses the natural right to pronounce the appellation "my Father"; he alone is truly Son.[6] "All things have been deliv-

---

6. Jesus cannot therefore serve as the paradigmatic "son" for humanity. His "references to 'my Father' and 'the Father/the Son' do not invite imitation. Jesus is not a

ered to me by my Father; and no one knows the Son except the Father, and no one knows the Father except the Son and any one to whom the Son chooses to reveal him" (Mt 11:27). Yet, Jesus also invites his disciples *to participate* in this filial relationship when he speaks to them of "your Father." "Let your light shine before men, that they may see your good works and give glory to your Father who is in heaven" (Mt 5:16).[7] This participatory status of his disciples is also found in the Lord's Prayer, since he teaches the disciples to address God as *"our* Father," thereby indicating that they do not have his unique privilege to address God as "my Father." Their sonship is communal, grounded in their discipleship; Jesus' sonship can be called natural, established in his very being.

The Fathers consistently teach that adoption takes place through the incarnation of God the Son, who united human and divine in himself. Thus, Christ deifies creation—renders it "like" God—and brings humanity into the trinitarian life. In a homily to catechumens, the fifth-century bishop Peter Chrysologus summarizes the significance of God's self-emptying and his union with fallen humanity: "And what is so surprising if he [Christ] consecrated humans as sons of God, when he gave himself and formed himself into the Son of Man? He carried the nature of the flesh into the divine when he brought divinity down to human nature. Then he offered man as an heir to himself in the heavens,

---

'typical' child of God. Others may use the language by invitation, not by imitation"; Donald Juel, "The Lord's Prayer in Matthew and Luke," in *The Lord's Prayer: Perspectives for Reclaiming Christian Prayer*, ed. Daniel Migliore (Grand Rapids, Mich.: Eerdmans, 1993), 60. For examples, see Mt 10:32–33, 12:50, 15:13, 16:17, 18:35, 20:23, 26:39, 26:53.

7. In particular, this relationship is formed through obedience to God's Word— "You, therefore, must be perfect, as your heavenly Father is perfect" (Mt 5:48)—and gift—"If you then, who are evil, know how to give good gifts to your children, how much more will your Father who is in heaven give good things to those who ask him" (Mt 7:11). For other examples, see Mt 5:44–45, 6:1, 10:20.

when he gave himself back as a participant in earthly things."[8] This *admirabile commercium*, the "miraculous exchange," that occurred in the union of two natures in the one person of Christ gives humanity a new and unmerited status as participants in the divine. Again, Peter Chyrsologus asks his catechumens, "What should inspire greater awe: that God gave himself to the earth, or that he gives you to heaven? That he himself enters into union with the flesh, or that he makes you enter into a union with divinity?"[9]

Jesus Christ makes this dynamic adoption possible through his birth, life, death, Resurrection, and Ascension. Augustine preaches, "And because we are called to an eternal inheritance in order that we might be coheirs of Christ and might come to the adoption as sons of God and since this is not from our own merits but from the grace of God, we put this same grace at the beginning of the prayer, when we say: 'our Father.'"[10] The seventh-century monk and theologian Maximus the Confessor also directs the faithful toward the *gift* of their new status: "We are also taught to speak to ourselves of the grace of adoption, since we are worthy to call Father by grace the one who is our Creator by nature."[11] One therefore does not *earn* the right to call God Father, but rather it is *given* to him through the generosity of the Creator.

This adoptive status finds its fulfillment in the sacrament of baptism. The fourth/fifth-century Syrian bishop Theodore of Mopsuestia, speaking in the voice of Christ himself—a rather

---

8. Peter Chrysologus, *Collectio sermonum* 70, ed. Alexander Olivar, CCL 24A (Turnhout: Brepols, 1981), 420, lines 14–17.

9. *Col. serm.* 67.2, CCL 24A, 402, lines 12–13.

10. Augustine of Hippo, *De sermone Domini in monte* II.4.16, ed. Almut Mutzenbecher, CCL 35 (Turnhout: Brepols, 1967), 106, lines 333–37.

11. Maximus the Confessor, *Expositio orationis dominicae*, ed. P. Van Deunn, CCG 23 (Turnhout: Brepols, 1991), 42, lines 259–63, in "Commentary on the Our Father," in *Maximus the Confessor: Selected Writings*, trans. George Berthold (New York: Paulist Press, 1985), 106.

presumptuous rhetorical practice for our modern ears—tells the recently baptized in his congregation:

Before everything else you should learn what you were and what is the nature and the measure of the gift that you received from God. The things that have happened to you are greater than those that happened to the children of men that were before you.... You have received through Me the grace of the Holy Spirit whereby you have obtained adoption of sons and confidence to call God, Father. You have not received the Spirit in order to be again in servitude and fear but to be worthy of the Spirit of adoption of sons through which you call God, Father, with confidence.[12]

After baptism, every Christian should, when reciting the Lord's Prayer, recall his own descent into the cleansing waters of the sacred font. The third-century bishop and martyr Cyprian of Carthage understands the prayer to be a personal declaration of the new life as a brother or sister of Christ: "Whoever therefore believes in his name is made a child of God, and hence should begin to give thanks and show himself a child of God as he names his Father as God in heaven. He bears witness also, among the first of his words at his rebirth, that he renounces his earthly and fleshly father and acknowledges that he has begun to have the Father in heaven as his only Father."[13] And John Cassian recalls the astonishing transformation that takes place in the baptized when he writes, "When, therefore, we confess with our own voice that the God and Lord of the universe is our Father, we profess that we have in fact been admitted from our servile condition into an adopted son-ship."[14]

12. Theodore of Mopsuestia, *Commentary on the Lord's Prayer*, in Theodore of Mopsuestia, *Commentary of Theodore of Mopsuestia on the Lord's Prayer and the Sacraments of Baptism and the Eucharist*, trans. Alphonse Mingana (Piscataway, N.J.: Gorgias, 2009), 6.

13. Cyprian of Carthage, *De oratione dominica* 9, PL 4, 525B, in *On the Lord's Prayer*, trans. Alistair Stewart-Sykes (Crestwood, N.Y.: St. Vladimir's Seminary Press, 2004), 71.

14. John Cassian, *Collationes* IX.18, in PL 49:789A, in John Cassian, *The Conferences*, trans. Boniface Ramsey, OP (New York: Newman Press, 1997), 341.

Though the Fathers consistently emphasized the efficacy of baptism for divine adoption, some believed that the Lord's Prayer itself could confer an anticipatory adoption for catechumens. Augustine, John Chrysostom, Theodore of Mopsuestia, and Peter Chrysologus followed the custom of "handing over" (*traditio*) the Lord's Prayer before the actual baptism, informing their charges that even in the preparatory period they could claim God as Father.[15] Thus, Augustine preaches to his anxious catechumens, "You see, you have begun to have God for your Father, and you will have Him when you are born anew. But *even now*, before you are born, you have been conceived of His seed, for you are about to be born of the font, which is, as it were, the womb of the Church. 'Our Father who are in heaven.' Remember that of your father Adam you have been born unto death, but of God the Father you will be reborn unto life."[16] Peter Chrysologus, in giving his catechumens Jesus' words, explains that "you have been elected today to the divine embryo, but you have not advanced; you know that you have arrived at the hope, but not the thing itself.... Today is the day of adoption, today is the time of the promise."[17] Hope and intention therefore empowered the catechumen to pronounce an anticipatory son-ship in the Lord's own words. He or she could call God "Father" because Jesus himself told them to "pray in this way."

For the earliest commentators, the Lord's Prayer therefore begins by recalling the gift of adoption effected in the incarnation

15. On fathers who performed the *traditio* of the Lord's Prayer prior to baptism, see Roy Hammerling, "The Lord's Prayer: A Cornerstone of Early Baptismal Education," in *A History of Prayer: The First to the Fifteenth Century*, ed. Roy Hammerling (Leiden: Brill, 2008), 167–82; Hammerling, *Lord's Prayer in the Early Church*, 69–70; Kenneth Stevenson, *The Lord's Prayer: A Text in Tradition* (Minneapolis: Fortress, 2004), 65–67.

16. Augustine of Hippo, *Serm.* 56.4.5, PL 38, column 375, in *Commentary on the Lord's Sermon on the Mount with Seventeen Related Sermons*, trans. Denis Kavanagh, OSA (New York: Fathers of the Church, 1951), 242.

17. Peter Chrysologus, *Col. serm.* 71.11, CCL 24A, 427–28, lines 97–103.

of the Son of God. This new relationship with God the Father finds its fulfillment in deification, the unification of the humanity and God that is analogous to the union of natures in the incarnation. Thus, the fourth-century bishop Cyril of Jerusalem could proclaim the depths of God's love for humanity: "O most surpassing loving-kindness of God! On them who revolted from Him and were in the very extreme of misery has He bestowed such complete forgiveness of their evil deeds, and so great participation of grace, as that they should even call Him Father."[18]

Growing in the Divine Likeness

Divine adoption is pure gift, and it cannot be earned; yet one must freely embrace and live up to the wonder of this great gift. In praying the Lord's Prayer, one *freely* takes on the Christ-Form, the full image of the Son: "What belongs to his own dignity, [Christ] wants to be under your own power: *As many as believed in him, he gave the power to become sons of God* (Jn 1:12)."[19] In fact, the recitation of the Lord's Prayer becomes the free appropriation of both one's adoption in baptism and baptism's concomitant responsibilities: by saying "Our Father," one declares to the world that he accepts the life of a child of God. The fourth-century bishop Chromatius of Aquileia teaches, "This is the pronouncement of freedom, full of assurance. Therefore, you must live by these morals in order that you might be sons of God and brothers of Christ.... Thus, show yourselves, most beloved, worthy of divine adoption.[20]

The children of God must grow in the virtues, which the Fathers consider to be reflections of divine qualities. Peter Chryso-

---

18. Cyril of Jerusalem, *Catecheses mystagogicae quinque* V.11, PG 33, 1117B, in *Lectures on the Christian Sacraments*, trans. F. L. Cross (Crestwood, N.Y.: St. Vladimir's Press, 1995), 75.

19. Peter Chrysologus, *Col. serm.* 69, CCL 24A, 416–17, lines 61–63.

20. Chromatius of Aquileia, *Sermon* 40.2, in *Chromace D'Aquilée*, ed. Joseph Lemarié, SC 154 (Paris: Cerf, 1971), 226, lines 21–28.

logus preaches, "That man demonstrates his divine sonship who is not overshadowed by human vices and shines with the divine virtues."[21] The saying "like Father, like son" becomes a mode of conduct for Christians, who strive to resemble their Creator. Maximus the Confessor writes, "Thus by respecting the designation of our Begetter in grace, we are eager to set on our life the features of the one who gave us life: We sanctify his name on earth in taking after him as a Father, in showing ourselves by our actions to be his children, and in extolling by our thoughts and our acts the Father's Son by nature, who is the one who brings about this adoption."[22]

Since Christians cannot "see" God, they must look toward Christ in order to imitate the divine virtues. Jesus, the perfect image of the Father, reveals the Father's qualities in a manner accessible to men. Origen of Alexandria explains how human beings can be children of God by growing in Christ's image through virtue or children of the devil by growing in the demonic image through vice:

Thus, the saints become an image of the image, since the image is the Son, and they are stamped with the sonship. They become conformed not only to the body of Christ's glory, but also to the One who is in the body. They become conformed to the One in the body of glory and are transformed by the renewal of the mind.... And just as the seed of God, when it remains in the one who has been begotten of God, causes the inability to sin because one has been transformed according to the only begotten Word, so in each one who sins there is the seed of the devil, to the extent that it dwells in the soul and prevents the one having it from doing right.[23]

21. Peter Chrysologus, *Col. serm.* 67.3, CCL 24A, 403, lines 30–31.
22. Maximus the Confessor, *Or. dom.*, CCG 23, 42, lines 263–68, in Berthold, *Maximus*, 106.
23. Origen of Alexandria, *De or.* 22, PG 11, 485B.

The Lord's Prayer therefore demands the formation of the believer: the baptized grow in the divine likeness through the appropriation of Christ's features. The ethical import of divine paternity inspires a Christian's entire life.

The Fathers also develop the social dimension of son-ship. They note that Jesus commands his disciples to pray "our Father," not "my Father." Prayer cannot be a selfish, individualist exercise, but must always acknowledge the communion of believers and the obligations toward that community. Cyprian, who lived in a Christian community fractured by persecution and betrayal, sought to inculcate the importance of unity in his congregation.[24] The Lord desired that the Church be one:

Before all else, the doctor of peace and the master of unity did not want prayer to become solitary and private, such that anyone, when he prays, only prays for himself. For we do not say, "*My* father who are in the heavens," nor, "Give *me* today my bread." Nor does each one request that only his own debt be remitted, nor does he ask that he alone not be led into temptation and freed from evil. For us, prayer is public and communal. And when we pray, we pray not for one, but for all people, because we are a whole people together as one. The God of peace and the master of concord, who taught unity, thus desired that one person pray for all in the same way that he himself carried all in one.[25]

A Christian should not consider his divine adoption to be a merited privilege or a reward for superior living. The baptismal font does not admit such arrogance or pride. "I do not wish you to say 'my' Father but 'our Father,' because He is a Father common to all in the same way as His grace, from which we received adoption of sons, is common to all. In this way you should not only offer congruous things to God, but you should also possess and keep

24. See Junghoo Kwon, "Cyprian, Origen and the Lord's Prayer: Theological Diversities between Latin West and Greek East in the Third Century," *Asia Journal of Theology* 26, no. 1 (April 2012): 57–58.

25. *De oratione dom.* 8, PL 4, 523B–24A.

fellowship with one another, because you are brothers and under the hand of one Father."[26] The regular recitation of the Lord's Prayer reminds the believer of his common inheritance as a child of God.

The Lord's Prayer therefore affects us: we become cognizant of our gifted status and its manner of life. The address "Our Father" should shock us. It should fill us with wonder and move us to reform. Augustine attempts to awaken his congregation to these truths:

> Furthermore, what great care touches one's mind as he says "Our Father," in order that he might not be unworthy of so great a Father! For if some plebian should be permitted by a senator of great estate to call him "father," the plebian undoubtedly will tremble and will not easily dare to do such a thing, thinking of the humble state of lineage, his lack of wealth and the meanness of his plebian person. Thus how much more must one fear calling God "Father," if there is so great a stain and such great uncleanness in his morals that God might be more just to expel the vices from his relationship, than a senator would justly expel the neediness of some beggar?[27]

Humanity has risen from the plebes to become royal sons and daughters. They share in the community found in the house of the Father.

Conclusion: Becoming Children of God

How, then, do the Fathers approach the twin problems of divine unknowability and human sinfulness? First, human beings know the Father because Jesus has revealed the Father to them, and he has invited them to participate in a relationship with the Father. Gregory of Nazianzus calls Christ "a concise and accessible rev-

---

26. Theodore of Mopsuestia, *Commentary on the Lord's Prayer*, trans. Mingana, 7.
27. *De serm. Dom.* II.4.16, CCL 35, 106, lines 344–53.

elation of the nature of the Father."[28] This is not to say that the mystery of God's very being has become subject to human analysis and control, but rather that Christ has made it possible for human beings to participate—in an analogous, but authentic, way—in his relationship with the Father. In becoming human, the Son opens up the gift of divine adoption to all, while also demonstrating the virtues that reflect divine qualities. Human beings call God Father because they know him through Christ and have been baptized in the Spirit. They rejoice in the greatest of all gifts—adoption into the trinitarian life.

It should be noted that the Fathers do not confront directly our contemporary concerns regarding the nature of fatherhood, such as the tragedy of absent fathers, abusive fathers, and other modern questions surrounding gender. Yet, one can discover an important insight in their discussion of Christ's revelation of the Father. We err when we try to project our notions of fatherhood onto God the Father. Such attempts may offer analogous images, but, in the end, they distort the depths of the divine mystery. Instead, we come to know what true fatherhood is through the Revelation in Jesus Christ. In other words, we should not drag the divine Father down to the human, but rather let grace elevate our human fathers up to the divine. Ronald Knox, the great Oxford scholar and priest, developed this insight in a homily on the Lord's Prayer:

How are we to recommend to them, then, as a model of all prayer the formula which begins with the words, Our Father? I think by pointing out to them that when we call God our Father we are not using metaphor; he is our Father in the full sense, not in some applied sense. When we call him a king, we mean that he is more of a king, not less of a king, than those earthly monarchs who share the title with him. Their sovereignty derives from his, not the other way around. So with

28. Gregory of Nazianzus, *Discourse* 30, in *Discours* 27–31, ed. P. Gallay, SC 250 (Paris: Cerf, 1978), 268, lines 11–12.

fatherhood; it is from God, St. Paul tells us, that all paternity in heaven and in earth is named.... It is only where and as they fall short of that perfect type that earthly fathers forfeit, in some degree, their title to paternity. You must not wait till you can learn to understand your father before you learn to know God. It is by learning to know God that you will learn to understand your Father.[29]

Jesus shows the Father to us: the Father is the one who is loving, but also the source of authority; the one who is compassionate, but also ready to rebuke his wayward children; the one who is always present, but also respects the freedom of his sons and daughters; the Creator of all who desires that his beloved creature might be with him. Human beings therefore can look toward Jesus' teachings to discover how they may be fathers; all may look toward Christ's revelation for the healing of their confused notions of fatherhood and manhood.

Second, the Fathers confront the problem of human sinfulness by turning this issue into a challenge: if human beings do not want to commit blasphemy in calling God "Father," they must strive to live up to the gift they have received. Calling God Father means living as genuine sons and daughters. If their lives do not reflect the life of the Father as demonstrated in the Son, they must reform their lives. No one who takes the writings of the Fathers of the Church to heart can recite the Lord's Prayer without reflecting upon the grave responsibilities that accompany the wondrous gift of adoption. A child of God has one mission in life: to become a saint worthy of the Father. The anonymous composer of the sixth-century monastic rule known as The Rule of the Master concludes, "For he who resembles his father not only in appearance but also in conduct is a true son."[30]

29. Ronald Knox, *Pastoral and Occasional Sermons* (San Francisco: Ignatius Press, 2002), 23–24.

30. *Regula magistri* [*La Régle du Maître*], ed. Adalbert de Vogüé, SC 105 (Paris: Cerf, 1964), 302, lines 73–76, in *The Rule of the Master*, trans. Luke Eberle (Collegeville, Minn.: Cistercian, 1977), 96.

Though the Fathers did not resolve this *aporia*, their insights point Christians toward deeper mysteries in the Lord's Prayer. "Our Father" calls for further reflection upon the nature of divine adoption, participation in Christian community, the nature of divine and human paternity, and the awesome responsibility of a filial relationship with God. All these things from just two words. Yet, one has only just begun the journey through Jesus' prayer. Even more awaits the sons and daughters of God.

3

SECOND *APORIA*

WHERE IS GOD THE FATHER?

Where is God? The popular imagination of the ancient and medieval world could still situate God in the upper regions of space,
where the realm of the stars and planets reflects the divine order.
God, though omnipresent in creation, still had a "place"—the
heavens that lay out of reach to earth-bound men and attested to
the Creator's presence.[1]

The Fathers, however, adamantly admonished their audiences
not to conceive of heaven as a *physical* place. Augustine preached
that, in prayer, "we turn toward the east, from where the heavens
rise. This is not to say that God dwells there, as if he should aban-

---

1. C. S. Lewis offers an exercise to aid the modern person in conceiving the
medieval cosmology—a cosmology grounded in ancient views: "You must go out
on a starry night and walk about for half an hour trying to see the sky in terms of the
old cosmology. Remember that you now have an absolute Up and Down. The Earth
is really the centre, really the lowest place; movement to it from whatever direction is downward movement. As a modern, you located the stars at a great distance.
From a distance you must now substitute that very special, and far less abstract, sort
of distance which we call height; height, which speaks immediately to our muscles
and nerves"; Lewis, *The Discarded Image* (Cambridge: Cambridge University Press,
2013), 98.

don certain parts of the world, since he is present everywhere—not in spatial intervals, but in the power of his majesty."[2] Origen of Alexandria also directed his readers away from such a simplistic reading of the Scriptures:

When the Father of the saints is said to be "in the heavens," it is not to be supposed that he is circumscribed by corporeal shape, and that so he dwells "in the heavens," for if the heavens contain him, it follows that God would be less than the heavens, whereas the ineffable power of his divinity entails our belief that all things are contained and held together by him.[3]

Yet, if heaven is not a space or place, what is it? *Where*, exactly, is God? How, Christians asked, could one find him?

"Heavens" or "Heaven"?

Before going to the commentaries of the Fathers, some important features of the Lord's Prayer require attention. First, the word "heaven" does not appear in Luke's version of the prayer, while "heaven" appears twice in Matthew's. Second, in the version of Matthew, the word appears in both the singular (*ouranos*) and plural form (*ouranoi*)—a fact that is lost in most translations. Thus, Matthew's version states, "Our Father, who are in the *heavens*, may your name be holy; your Kingdom come, your will be done, on earth as it is in *heaven*." The version of the *Didache*, however, changes the plural form to a singular, as we find in modern translations: "Our Father who are in heaven."

Is there any significance in the use of plural and singular? Scholars have various positions on this problem. I will consider one compelling approach here that helps to illuminate the Fathers' treatment of "heaven" and the location of God.

2. *De serm. Dom.* II.5.18, CCL 35, 108, lines 383–86.
3. *De or.* 23, PG 11, 485D, in Stewart-Sykes, *Lord's Prayer*, 162.

"Heaven and Earth": The Created Cosmos

The couplet "heaven and earth" often appears in Matthew to designate the created cosmos. In these examples, "heaven" refers to the upper realm of created beings—the sky, the visible stars, angels—while "earth" embraces the lower regions—the created things of our world, as well as the dead in nether-regions of Gehenna.[4] Thus the couplet serves as a euphemism for the entirety of the created cosmos. For example:

Truly I say to you, till heaven and earth pass away, not an iota, not a dot, will pass from the law until all is accomplished. (Mt 5:18)

Heaven and earth will pass away, but my words will not pass away. (Mt 24:35)

And Jesus came and said to them, "All Authority in heaven and on earth has been given to me." (Mt 28:18)

The Father therefore has authority over "heaven and earth"—that is, over all the things that emerged from his act of creation. Yet, the Father shares this authority with the Son. The incarnate Son proclaims that the same authority has been given to him; he too reigns over the upper and lower regions of the cosmos (Mt 28:18).

Heavens: The Transcendence of the Father

When speaking of God the Father, Matthew most often uses the plural "heavens," as opposed to the singular "heaven." In this case, the kingdom of the Heavens points toward the Father's wholly other order of existence. For example:

And call no man your father on earth, for you have one Father, who is in the heavens. (Mt 23:9)

I will give you the keys of the kingdom of the heavens, and whatever you bind on earth shall be bound in the heavens, and whatever you loose on earth shall be loosed in the heavens. (Mt 16:19)

---

4. Jonathan T. Pennington, *Heaven and Earth in the Gospel of Matthew* (Ada, Mich.: Baker Academic, 2009), 208–9.

In these two instances, "the heavens" designates not the created "heaven" or a place—stars, upper regions—but the otherness of God the Father, as well as the Father's radical holiness.[5]

This absolute holiness of the heavens, the transcendence of God, does not mean, however, that the Father has no relationship with creation. The Father in the heavens, in fact, shares in an intimate relationship with humanity and creation. The divide between "heavens" and "heaven and earth" does not imply the deist's God, a separate and aloof being, but rather it highlights the Father's stunning choice to share his life with his own creation. Many verses express this intimate relationship with the God who wants his creatures to share in his life. For example:

Love your enemies and pray for those who persecute you, so that you may be sons of your Father who is in the heavens. (Mt 5:45)

If you then, who are evil, know how to give good gifts to your children, how much more will your Father who is in heavens give good things to those who ask him! (Mt 7:11)

So it is not the will of my Father who is in the heavens that one of these little ones should perish. (Mt 18:14)

Though "the heavens" serve as a euphemism for the transcendent Lord, the Father desires to unite the uncreated and created: "Blessed are the poor in spirit, for theirs is the kingdom of the heavens" (Mt 5:3).

Uniting "the Heavens" with "Earth and Heaven"

The Lord's Prayer conveys the desire for the unification of the created and the divine. This becomes clearer in the three petitions enclosed between "heavens" and "heaven:"[6]

---

5. "The term 'heaven[s]' is a Jewish substitute for 'God' (see 1 Maccabees), apparently intended to avoid using the term 'God' too freely"; Daniel Harrington, *The Gospel of Matthew* (Collegeville, Minn.: Liturgical Press, 2007), 79.

6. W. D. Davies and D. C. Allison highlight this distinct unit of the prayer: "Note that οὐρανῷ creates an *inclusio* with the οὐρανοῖς of 9b and thus separates the

Our Father who are in *the Heavens* [Creator]
(1) Let your name be hallowed [Petition]
(2) Let your kingdom come [Petition]
(3) Let your will be done [Petition]
On *earth* as it is in *heaven* [Creation]

The unit encloses three petitions between the Father in the *heavens*—that is, the Glory of God the Creator who is wholly other—and *heaven and earth*—that is, the created cosmos. Thus, a bridge is formed between Creator and creation through the fulfillment of three petitions: the hallowing of God's name, the inbreaking of the kingdom, and the fulfillment of the divine will. A unity is formed not between two *places*, but between the transcendent holiness of God and the created cosmos.

The Fathers on "Heaven/Heavens"

The Fathers rarely comment on the "heavens/heaven" distinction, and some work with a version of the prayer that has only the singular form. Yet, they do acknowledge the difference between the uncreated "heaven of the Father" and celestial regions of "heaven and earth." Furthermore, despite lacking the clear distinction been "heavens" and "heaven," they nonetheless do develop the significant themes discussed earlier. In fact, the Fathers generally focus on three points when addressing the problem of God the Father's place: divine transcendence; the unification of creation with the divine; and heaven as the goal of the Christian's earthly pilgrimage.

Heaven Designates Divine Transcendence

At the beginning of this chapter I noted that the Fathers did not believe that "the heavens" of the Father were a physical place. Au-

first half of the prayer from the last half"; Davies and Allison, *Matthew 1–7* (New York: T. and T. Clark, 2004), 1:606.

gustine, for instance, does not situate God in the upper regions of the created cosmos: "But if the place of God is believed to be in the heavens as in the higher parts of the world, the birds would be of greater merit, since their life is closer to God."[7] Augustine instead makes a distinction between the spatial realms of "earth and heaven" and the "heaven's heaven," which designates God's *transcendent* glory. He writes in the *Confessions*:

But where, Lord, is that *heaven's heaven* of which we hear in the psalm: *Heaven's heaven is for the Lord; but he has assigned the earth to human-kind* (Ps 113:16). Where is that heaven we cannot see, in comparison with which all we can see is but earth? This whole material world has been endowed with beauty of form in its furthest parts, the lowest of which is our earth (though not uniformly throughout, for the material world is not the same or wholly present everywhere); yet compared with *heaven's heaven* the heaven that overarches our earth is itself no better than earth. And without good reason, are those two vast reali-ties—our earth and our sky—to be regarded as mere lowly earth beside that unimaginable heaven which is for the Lord, not for humankind.[8]

God is other than the physical world and heaven, since he exists outside of its confines as the Creator. Origen wrote, "'Our Father who are in the heavens' … sets apart the essence of God from all begotten beings."[9] Peter Chrysologus, in the fifth centu-ry, echoed this position: "When you say 'Our Father, who are in the heavens,' do not say it as if he were not here on earth, but do not receive it as if [the Father] were enclosed in a place—the One who encloses all things."[10] "Heavens" in the Lord's Prayer acts as the corrective to the erroneous containment of God in creation and recognizes God as transcendent and wholly other.

---

7. *De serm. Dom.* II.5.17, CCL 35, 107, lines 367–70.
8. Augustine of Hippo, *The Confessions*, trans. Maria Boulding, OSB (New York: New City Press, 1997), 312–13.
9. *De or.* 23.5, PG 11, 489D–91A, in Stewart-Sykes, *Lord's Prayer*, 165.
10. *Col. serm.* 67, CCL 24A, 403, lines 26–29.

Uniting Creation with the Transcendent God

Since God is wholly other, an untraversable divide separates creation from God. Even apart from the deleterious divisions caused by sin,[11] creation cannot ascend to union with God on its own initiative. Origen writes, "Then there is this passage from Ecclesiastes: 'Do not rush to bear your word before God, because God is in the heaven above and you are on the earth below (Eccl 5:2).' It wishes to make clear the distance between beings that are in the body of humility, and the angels that are elevated by the aid of the Word, and the holy powers, and Christ himself."[12]

Yet, the grace of divine adoption—the grace in calling God "Father"—has established a new dynamic in humanity. Through gift and cooperation, the Christian becomes a citizen of the heavens of the Father. This does not mean that he has entered or will enter a new "place," but rather that he shares in the trinitarian life and that he may no longer give allegiance to earthly things. Theodore of Mopsuestia, in the fourth century, addresses the catechumens in the voice of Jesus himself: "I added 'which art in heaven,' so that the figure of the life in heaven, to which it has been granted to you to be transferred, might be drawn before your eyes. When you have received the adoption of sons, you will dwell in heaven, and this abode is fit for the sons of God."[13] The heavens are therefore both a new spiritual state for the baptized Christian in this life—the new life in the Spirit—*and* a fullness of life that is to come in the resurrection.

One can see evidence of this new citizenship in the way the

---

11. Gregory of Nyssa, in his homilies on the Beatitudes, describes the harsh inequalities and warring factions that mar human existence as a result of sin: "Life is in many ways divided up into opposites, since it may be spent as slave or as master, in riches or poverty, in fame or dishonor, in bodily infirmity or in good health—in all such things there is division"; *Beat.* 5, GNO 7.2, 126, lines 8–11, in Graef, *Lord's Prayer*, 132.

12. *De or.* 23.4, PG 11:489D.

13. Theodore of Mopsuestia, *Commentary on the Lord's Prayer*, trans. Mingana, 8.

Christian lives. Cyprian of Carthage wrote, "We who have begun to be spiritual and heavenly, should think and perform spiritual and heavenly things."[14] Augustine understands this union to be effected when the body—earth—integrates itself with the spirit—heaven:

> This is also in no way absurd and is understood most appropriately in respect to our faith and hope that we may accept heaven and earth to be spirit and flesh ... this means that, just as the spirit, by following and doing his will, does not resist God, so the body does not resist the spirit, or the soul, which is now agitated by the infirmity of the body and is inclined toward fleshly habits.[15]

In general, these Fathers highlight an already effective adoption at work in the Christian. In a sense, the Christian is not of this world, or earth, but already shares in the divine life that forms a new mode of existence.

Maximus the Confessor, in his commentary on the Lord's Prayer, highlights the ascetic dimension of this heavenly citizenship:

> The one who mystically offers God worship through the spiritual power alone separated from concupiscence and anger has accomplished the will of God on earth as the angelic orders do in heaven. He has become in every way the companion of the angels in their worship and in their life, as the great Apostle somewhere says, "Our citizenship is in heaven," where there is no concupiscence to relax the mind's reach by pleasures, nor raging anger to bark indecently against one's kinsmen, but where there will be reason all by itself to lead naturally rational beings to the first Principle. It is this alone which gladdens God and which God requests of us his servants.[16]

The ascetic life—a life of self-denial, struggle against vices, and growth in virtue—renders one *isangelos*, "equal to an angel," and

---

14. *De oratione dom.* 11, PL 4, 526C, in Stewart-Sykes, *Lord's Prayer*, 72.
15. *De serm. Dom.* II.6.23, CCL 35, 112–13, lines 484–86 and 492–96.
16. *Or. dom.*, CCG 23, 57, lines 521–31, in Berthold, *Maximus*, 112.

it becomes a participation in the spiritual life. Separation from concupiscence (*epithumia*), the font of disordered desires, and wrath (*thumos*), the source of rashness and violence, allows the spiritual power of reason (*logos*) to reorder the fallen soul in conformity with the divine image. The person shaped by reason (*logos*) will then seek union with the divine Word or Principle (*Logos*), thereby entering the heavenly, spiritual state.[17]

The Pilgrimage toward Heaven

Though the Fathers consistently taught that the heavens were not a physical place, they did use metaphorical spatial language to make heaven the goal of the Christian journey. Heaven becomes the shrine that the weary Christian pilgrim seeks.

On the one hand, Augustine uses a spatial metaphor to show how the just already share in heavenly citizenship: in a way, when God indwells the saint, the saint's soul becomes heaven and the dwelling place of God: "'For the temple of God is holy, because you are holy' (1 Cor 3:16). Thus if God dwells in his temple and the saints are his temple, it is right to say that the one who is in

17. Elsewhere, Maximus brings out the communal and cosmological import of man's unification with heaven. The divisions that mar creation exist because man, the principle of unity in God's creation, turned away from God and preferred the selfish exploitation of a fragmented world. Christ, in becoming man, effects the mediations between the divisions of the cosmos and reestablishes man's participation in this mission of unification. Maximus outlines an itinerary for man, who is called "to achieve within himself the mode of their completion, and so bring to light the great mystery of the divine plan, realizing in God the union of the extremes which exist among beings, by harmoniously advancing in an ascending sequence from the proximate to the remote and from the inferior to the superior." The divisions that Christ healed and that man must also unite are, in order of ascent: male and female; paradise and the inhabited world; heaven and earth; intelligible and sensible; and uncreated and created. Man, therefore, participates in a healing of divisions not only for *himself*, but also *for the entire cosmos*: the one who shattered God's creation may, through Christ, participate in its restoration and intimate union with God; Maximus the Confessor, *Ambiguum* 41, in *On Difficulties in the Church Fathers: The "Ambigua,"* ed., trans. Nicholas Constas (Cambridge, Mass.: Harvard University Press, 2014), 2:104–5.

the heavens is, in fact, in the saints."[18] Thus, though spatial dimensions do not limit God, God nonetheless comes to abide in the lives of the holy ones, thereby rendering their souls "heaven."[19] When one recites the Lord's Prayer, the Father in the heavens enters one's soul:

Therefore "Our Father who are in the heavens" is rightly understood to say that he [the Father] is in the hearts of the just as if within his holy temple. Also, at the same time, he who prays also wants the One he invokes to also dwell within his very self. When he strives for this, he desires to hold fast to justice, and by this duty God is invited to dwell in the mind.[20]

On the other hand, the Fathers also highlight the spiritual journey toward the heavens—to a fuller union with God—as the Christian goal. Gregory of Nyssa gives heaven a metaphorical "place" marker by calling it "home." It is the spiritual Paradise that man abandoned at the beginning, just as the prodigal son abandoned his Father's house.[21] This home does not acquire a physical location for Gregory, but it does involve a reorientation of humanity *from* this fallen world of self-exile *toward* the life of God the Father. The prodigal Christian therefore journeys away from spatial confinement, with all its blandishments, toward the spiritual "place" intended by God:

Thus, the return of the young man to his Father's home became to him the occasion of experiencing the loving kindness of his Father; for this

18. *De serm. Dom.* II.5.17, CCL 35, 107, lines 376–77.

19. Cyril of Jerusalem shares this view. "They also, too, are a heaven who bear the image of the heavenly, in whom God is 'dwelling and walking in them' (2 Cor 6:16)"; Cyril of Jerusalem, *Catecheses* V.11, PG 33:1117B, in Cross, *Lectures*, 75.

20. *De serm. Dom.* II.5.18, CCL 35, 108, lines 403–8.

21. Gregory therefore seems to identify "heaven" with the original Paradise of man. This upward, or anagogical, movement means a return to an original state. The problematic implications of an Origenian "preexistence" of souls is genuine. On these issues see Hans Boersma, *Embodiment and Virtue in Gregory of Nyssa: An Analogical Approach* (Oxford: Oxford University Press, 2015), 44–50.

paternal home is the Heaven against which, as he says to his Father, he has sinned. In the same way it seems to me that if the Lord is teaching us to call upon the Father in Heaven, He means to remind you of our beautiful fatherland.[22]

Thus, when we make the heavens of the Father the goal of our journey, we already liberate ourselves from dependence upon a deceptive world and rediscover the freedom of Paradise.[23] Though Gregory's understanding of heaven as a "return" for man is not without its problematic implications, his interpretation provides his audience with a spiritual "direction": if God is our Father, we belong in his house.[24] Heaven is our home.

The monastic founder John Cassian, in the fifth century, also made heaven the longed-for shrine of the Christian pilgrim:

Then we add: "Who are in heaven," so that, avoiding with utter horror the dwelling place of the present life, wherein we sojourn on this earth as on a journey and are kept at a far distance from our Father, we may instead hasten with great desire to that region in which we say that our Father dwells and do nothing that would make us unworthy of this profession of ours and of the nobility of so great an adoption.[25]

In the fourth century John Chrysostom, the renowned preacher and bishop, spoke of the reorientation of humanity toward a higher spiritual union. The conversion of humanity toward the heavens will forge a new community. Since God is *our* Father— not just *my* Father—heaven will be a state of communion:

But when He said, "in Heaven," He speaks not this as shutting up God there, but as withdrawing him who is praying from earth, *and fixing him*

22. *De or. dom.* 2, GNO 7.2, 27, lines 24–29, in Graef, *Lord's Prayer*, 42.

23. "No longer do we go astray, pinning our hope on what is unstable and subject to change. For earth is the place of variation and flux ... but by saying Kingdom of Heaven He shows the absolute immutability of the gift that is held out to our expectation"; *Beat.* 8, GNO 7.2, 162, lines 7–8 and 17–18, in Graef, *Lord's Prayer*, 167.

24. "In my Father's house there are many rooms" (Jn 14:2).

25. *Col.* IX.18, PL 49, 789A, in Ramsey, *Conferences*, 341.

in the high places, and in the dwellings above.... For what harm comes of kindred below, when in that which is on high we are all of us knit together, and no one has more than another; neither the rich more than the poor, nor the master than the servant, neither the ruler than the subject, nor the king than the common soldier, nor the philosopher than the barbarian, nor the skillful than the unlearned? For to all has He given one nobility, having vouchsafed to be called the Father of all alike.[26]

These Fathers avoid anthropomorphizing God by refusing to situate him in a physical place. Instead, they use the metaphor of space to reorient the human person toward God the Father and a higher state of union with him. The new relationship with the Father requires a journey from earth to heaven, from sin to freedom in grace.

Conclusion: A Pilgrimage to Heaven

The Lord's Prayer contains a dynamic movement toward the union of creation with God. The transcendent Father of the heavens reaches out to the created order of heaven and earth. This movement will become more evident with the examination of additional *aporiai* in the light of the Fathers' wisdom.

The Fathers address the problem of "the heavens" by making it a designation for divine transcendence and holiness. Yet, in light of the incarnation, they are not content to isolate the loving Creator from humanity. In keeping with the dynamic of the prayer, they emphasize that the adopted children of God have acquired citizenship in the heavens—that is, the sons and daughters are to traverse the divide between the created and the Creator through grace and spiritual growth. The heavenly Father indwells

26. John Chrysostom, *Homiliae in Matthaeum*. Vol. 1, Homily 19, ed. F. Field (Cambridge: Officina Academica, 1839), 277; *The Homilies of St. John Chrysostom on the Gospel of Matthew*, trans. S. G. Prevost (Oxford: J. H. Parker, 1843), 293. Translation adapted.

the souls of the just, and the saints journey daily toward their true goal: union with God the Father.

This *aporia* therefore inspires the Christian to become a pilgrim. He or she cannot remain content with celestial and earthly goals, but instead focuses upon the *unum necessarium*: coming to live in the house of the Father. This reorientation of one's existence demands reassessment of priorities, a dedication of will, and growth in charity toward God and neighbor. A pilgrimage is an arduous journey—especially when it is the journey into God. Yet, the Father in the heavens will bestow all necessary graces, and the humble pilgrim will be drawn by the power of love.

4

THIRD *APORIA*

HOW CAN GOD GROW IN HOLINESS?

Is Anything Sacred?

We live in a time when nothing is sacred. Our age takes great pride in making all things mundane; the aura of holiness can no longer protect any person or place from public derision. As the secular lays claim to ever-greater swaths of personal and public life, the sacred flees to silent, forgotten temples and tabernacles, while modern man vainly strives to fill the spiritual void with chemical bliss and vapid entertainment.

The holiness of the divine name has also faded from our collective memory. We have drained it of its power to inspire, frighten, and transform by repeatedly inserting it into the context of the profane and the banal. Yet this sacredness demands recovery. "It is possible for everything and everyone on earth to forget the sanctity of God and his name.... It is thus important constantly to renew our recognition of the holiness of his name, to call it to mind."[1]

1. Holger Zaborowski, "'Hallowed Be Thy Name': Of God and Men and the Miracle of Language," *Communio* 43, no. 1 (2016): 14. Also see Black, *Lord's Prayer*, 84–92.

But how can this be? Can creatures actually rob the Creator's name of its holiness? It would appear that the first petition of the Lord's Prayer calls for a restoration or an increase of divine holiness—a strange request that did not go unnoticed by the Fathers. "Indeed, how could God, who is himself the one who hallows, be hallowed?" asks Cyprian.[2] And Augustine presents these questions to his catechumens: "Why should you ask that the name of God be hallowed? It is holy. Why then, do you ask for the hallowing of what is already holy?"[3]

The Holiness of God's Name in the Scriptures

What's in a Name?

For the ancients, a name conveyed the very being or essence of its referent.[4] "To know, understand, the name of a person was to know the person himself."[5] It is God who most truly has the power to name *and* give being, as evinced in the creation story from the book of Genesis: "God called the light Day and the darkness he called Night. And there was evening and there was morning, one day" (Gn 1:5ff). And when God gives a person a new name, that person changes in the core of his being and a new relationship is established: Abram became Abraham, the father of his people (Gn 17:5); Jacob, he who had "striven with God and with men, and prevailed," became Israel (Gn 32:28). One could not separate the name from the mystery of the one named.

The Hebrew people received the unique gift of knowing God's name. The unfathomable mystery of God could not be reduced to a single term that enclosed his essence; yet, at the same time,

---

2. *De oratione dom.* 12., PL 4, 527A, in Stewart-Sykes, *Lord's Prayer*, 73.

3. Augustine of Hippo, *Serm.* 56.5, PL 38, 379, in Kavanagh, *Commentary*, 243.

4. Jean Carmignac, *Recherches sur le Notre Père* (Paris: Letouzey and Ane, 1969), 79; Ernst Lohmeyer, *"Our Father": An Introduction to The Lord's Prayer*, trans. J. Bowden (New York: Harper Collins, 1965), 74.

5. Albright and Mann, *Matthew*, 75.

God's self-revelation from the burning bush established an intimate relationship with the Creator:

Then Moses said to God, "If I come to the sons of Israel and say to them, 'The God of your fathers has sent me to you,' and they ask me, 'What is his name?' what shall I say to them?" God said to Moses, "*I am who I am.*" And he said, "Say this to the sons of Israel, '*I am* has sent me to you.'" God also said to Moses, "Say this to the sons of Israel, '*The Lord, the God of your fathers*, the God of Abraham, the God of Isaac and the God of Jacob, has sent me to you': this is my name for ever and thus I am to be remembered throughout all generations" (Ex 3:13–15).

"I am," "ʏᴡʜᴡ"—the letters that designate the name of "Yahweh—the Lord," "the God of your Fathers": these names do not make God an object in the created world, but they do mark a radical entrance of God into history. A particular people, in a particular place, and in a particular time came to know God in his self-gift. "In this revelation, he shows us that he himself has a proper name; he is not something, but someone, and his name is a pledge, a promise. For God reveals himself as one who is there for man."[6] The name of God transforms the narrative of history, since Israel now knows this name and receives the protection and guidance of the one true God: "But I acted *for the sake of my name*, that it should not be profaned in the sight of the nations among whom they dwelt, in whose sight I made myself known to them in bringing them out of the land of Egypt" (Ez 20:9).

Yet with this name came a great mission, since the God of Israel is the All-Holy One, superior in being and in act. Moses demonstrated his awe by removing his shoes in order to approach the great theophany, the revelation of God, and receive the divine name (Ex 3:5–6). The Lord's name is never to be taken in vain, nor may it be tainted by the worship of foreign gods: "You shall not give any of your children to devote them by force to

6. Zaborowski, "Hallowed Be Thy Name," 13.

Molech, and so profane *the name of your God*: I am the Lord"
(Lv 18:21). Israel was therefore missioned to glorify God's name
in the world through an *imitatio Dei*, a manifestation of God's
holiness through their practice of holiness.[7] When the Hebrew
people lived by God's precepts, there would be blessings: "*They
will sanctify my name*; they will sanctify the Holy One of Jacob,
and will stand in awe of the God of Israel" (Is 29:23). But when
they profaned God's name through injustice and moral pollution,
they would be called back through harsh trials and exile: "But
when they came to the nations, wherever they came, *they profaned my holy name*, in that men said of them, 'These are the people of the Lord, and yet they had to go out of his land.' But I had
concern for my holy name, which the house of Israel caused to be
profaned among the nations to which they came" (Ez 36:20–21).
All would come to know the holiness of the divine name through
the manner of life seen in the Chosen People:

So you shall keep my commandments and do them: I am the Lord.
*And you shall not profane my holy name, but I will be hallowed among
the sons of Israel*; I am the Lord who sanctify you, who brought you
out of the land of Egypt to be your God: I am the Lord. (Lv 22: 31–33)

God's name, the *tetragrammaton*—the four Hebrew letters,
yōd, hê, wāw, hê that form the name YHWH—acquired an ever-
greater sense of holiness, especially during Israel's periods of exile and oppression. Various circumlocutions, such as *Adonai*, or
Lord, were used as substitutes in order to avoid pronouncing the
sacred name YHWH.[8] For example, the ancient synagogue prayer

7. The understanding of this *imitatio Dei* would undergo development especially during Israel's long years of exile and occupation. This concern with holiness
became the preservation of identity amidst the temptations to conform. "Yahweh
was holy and Yahweh's people, living by an *imitatio Dei*, were to be holy"; see Marcus
Borg, *Conflict, Holiness and Politics in the Teachings of Jesus* (Harrisburg, Pa.: Trinity
Press International, 1998), 76.

8. See R. Kendall Soulen, "Hallowed Be Thy Name! The Tetragrammaton and

called the Kaddish, in which one finds elements of the Lord's Prayer, points toward the hallowed name without pronouncing the divine name itself:

> May his *great name* be exalted and sanctified in the world, which he made according to his will. May his kingdom rule, his redemption spring forth, may he bring near his Messiah and save his people, in your lifetime, in your days, in the lifetime of all the house of Israel, quickly and soon. And you shall say, "Amen."[9]

The holiness of God's name, the *tetragrammaton*, in fact "points irresistibly forward to the consummation of God's universal rule, when there will be an end to the state in which 'all day long my name is despised' (Is 52:5), and God's incomparable uniqueness will be fittingly honored by Israel, the nations, and all creation."[10]

Honoring "the Name" in Matthew and Luke

The hallowing of the divine name stands out in the New Testament in various forms. For instance, Jesus himself often uses the circumlocution called the "divine passive," in which the passive voice points toward God as the actor without pronouncing his name: "Judge not that you *be not judged* [by God]" (Mt 7:1); "for everyone who exalts himself *will be humbled* [by God], but he who humbles himself *will be exalted* [by God] (Lk 18:14)"; "But after *I am raised up* [by the Father], I will go before you to Galilee" (Mt 36: 32).[11] Another example would be the title *kyrios*, Lord, which also became a substitute for the divine name.[12] By Christian times, the Greek Old Testament, the *Septuagint*, had

---

the Name of the Trinity," in *Jews and Christians: People of God*, ed. Carl Braaten and Robert Jenson (Grand Rapids, Mich.: Eerdmans, 2003), 22.

9. Cited in Albright and Mann, *Matthew*, 76. Also see Harrington, *Matthew*, 95.

10. Soulen, "Hallowed Be Thy Name!," 22.

11. Soulen, "Hallowed Be Thy Name!," 23–25.

12. See Charles Gieschen, "The Divine Name in Ante-Nicene Christology," *Vigiliae Christianae* 57, no. 2 (2003): 116–21.

replaced all references to the *tetragrammaton* with abbreviations of *kurios* or *theos*, and this practice found its way into the New Testament writings.[13] Thus John the Baptist applies Isaiah 30:3 to the coming of Jesus: "The voice of one crying in the wilderness: Prepare the way of *the Lord*, make his paths straight" (Mt 3:3), and the Apostles proclaim the risen Jesus by saying, "*The Lord* has risen indeed, and has appeared to Simon!" (Lk 24:34).

Most importantly, we find Jesus' references to "the name." In the Gospel of Matthew, in which one version of the Lord's Prayer is found, "the name" has multiple meanings. In one verse, the divine name is applied to the Trinity: "Go therefore and make disciples of all nations, baptizing them *in the name* of the Father and of the Son and of the Holy Spirit" (Mt 28:19). In other verses, Jesus applies this "name," which is hallowed and bears power, to himself. For example, "Whoever receives one such child *in my name* receives me" (Mt 18:5). Charles Gieschen notes that "this is not a reference to the personal name 'Jesus'; it is a reference to the Divine Name possessed by Jesus that is also possessed by the Father and the Holy Spirit."[14] Other examples of this use include:

And you will be hated by all *for my name's sake*. (Mt 10:22)

For where two or three are gathered *in my name*, there am I in the midst of them. (Mt 18:20)

And every one who has left houses or brothers or sisters or father or mother or children or lands, *for my name's sake*, will receive a hundred-fold and inherit eternal life. (Mt 19:29)

The divine name is associated with Jesus; both he and the Spirit are identified with the name above all names.

---

13. Regarding the scholarship and controversies surrounding the use of *kyrios* and other circumlocutions in both Jewish and Christian Greek texts, see Robert Wilkinson, *Tetragrammaton: Western Christians and the Hebrew Name of God* (Boston: Brill, 2015), 50–65, 90–116. Also see Larry Hurtado, *Lord Jesus Christ: Devotion to Jesus in Earliest Christianity* (Grand Rapids, Mich.: Eerdmans), 20–21.

14. Gieschen, "Divine Name," 146.

Luke also develops a theology surrounding "the name," especially in the Acts of the Apostles.[15] Two themes come to the fore: the application of the divine name to Jesus and the association of this name with Jesus' disciples. Thus, Peter proclaims, "And it shall be that whoever calls *on the name of the Lord* shall be saved" (Acts 2:21). The believer is united with the name of Jesus in baptism: "Repent, and be baptized every one of you *in the name of Jesus Christ* for the forgiveness of your sins; and you shall receive *the gift of the Holy Spirit*" (Acts 2:38). The disciple in turn comes to accept all things belonging to "the name," including suffering: "Then Paul answered, 'What are you doing, weeping and breaking my heart? For I am ready not only to be imprisoned but even to die at Jerusalem *for the name of the Lord Jesus*'" (Acts 21:13). Before the great signs being worked in the Church, "*the name of the Lord Jesus was extolled*" (Acts 19:17).[16] The name of Jesus holds the power of the divine, while the disciple who lives and dies in that name receives life.

The Fathers Hallow the Divine Name

The Sacred Name

Origen of Alexandria gives a profound explanation of the significance of a proper name. A proper name, unlike a generic name for an object, embraces all the unique qualities of a person and distinguishes that person from all others. The changing of a name therefore implies a change in the substantiating qualities of the person:

Now a name is a summary designation indicative of the proper quality of the thing named. Thus, the apostle Paul has proper quality, that of his soul, which is of a certain kind; that of his mind, which contem-

15. Gieschen, "Divine Name," 146–48.
16. For an overview of the cultic invocation of Jesus' name, particularly in Pauline Christianity, see Hurtado, *Lord Jesus Christ*, 197–206.

plates particular things, and that of his body, which is of a certain kind. Now what is peculiar to these properties and not shared by anybody else is designated by the name "Paul," for there is no being in existence identical with Paul. But in the case of persons whose particular qualities, so to speak, alter, their names, according to Scripture, are quite rightly altered. Thus when the quality of Abram altered, he was called "Abraham," and in the case of Simon he was called "Peter," and in the case of Saul, the persecutor of Jesus, he was called "Paul." But in the case of God, insofar as he is himself unchangeable, and is eternally unalterable, the name that, so to speak, he bears is one, that which is mentioned in Exodus, "He who is," or words to that effect (Ex 3:14).[17]

Though human proper names can change in order to designate qualitative changes—a conversion, a new mission, a new state of life—God's name holds the *permanence* of his Being. This name therefore acts as God's unalterable presence in history; its pronunciation invokes the One who remains faithful to his covenant and promises. Human beings must honor the power of this name gifted through the revelation of the Scriptures. Peter Chrysologus proclaimed, "Brothers, this name is what the highest powers fear, what they defend with the most fearful servitude; this name is what puts demons to flight; this name alone is what frees souls that are captive to the savageness of the devil; this is the name that gives salvation to a lost world."[18]

Some Fathers identify the name that is to be hallowed not with God the Father, but with the Son. "For the name of God the Father who subsists essentially *is the only-begotten Son*."[19] Jesus not only reveals the Father's name, he demonstrates that his own name is equal with that of the Father. To honor the divine name is also to honor Jesus Christ: "The name of God the Father had been revealed to nobody. Even Moses, who had asked it of God himself, heard of a different name (Ex 3:14–15). But to us it is

17. *De or.* 24.2, PG 11, 492B, in Stewart-Sykes, *Lord's Prayer*, 166.
18. *Col. serm.* 71.4, CCL 24A, 425, lines 42–46.
19. *Or. dom.*, CCG 23, 41, lines 239–40, in Berthold, *Maximus*, 106.

revealed in the Son, for now we know that 'Son' is the new name of the Father. 'I have come,' he said, 'in the name of the Father (Jn 5:43). And more openly: 'I have made your name known to people'" (Jn 12:6).[20]

The Meaning of Holiness

What do the Fathers mean by holiness? St. John Chrysostom equates holiness with glory. To "hallow" God therefore means to praise him, to acknowledge his glory: "Worthy of him who calls God Father, is the prayer to ask nothing before the glory of His Father, but to account all things secondary to the work of praising Him. For 'hallowed' is 'glorified.'"[21]

Origen teaches that, because of God's transcendence, human beings can never truly bear the full weight of divine holiness. Instead, they receive a sense of this holiness through God's activities in creation: we do not know *what* God is, but God's generous activity on our behalf proves him to be holy. Holiness therefore designates an array of works that belong uniquely to the Creator:

Thus all, on the one hand, have conceived something about God, having certain things about him in their minds; yet, on the other hand, not all know *what* he is—for few, or better to say, the fewest of few, grasp his holiness in all its aspects. Therefore, we are rightly taught a conception of God as "holy," in order that we might see the holiness of one who creates, orders providentially, judges, elects, abandons, welcomes and rejects, and rewards and punishes each one according to his merit.[22]

The disparaging of holiness, blasphemy, consists of actions that detract from God's *philanthropia*—that is, from God's love for humanity. Human beings acquire a limited understanding of God's holiness by contemplating his works; they obscure God's holiness through the blasphemy of sin. Human holiness there-

20. *De oratione* 3, PL 1, 1155A–56A, in Stewart-Sykes, *Lord's Prayer*, 43.
21. *In Matthaeum* IX.278, in Prevost, *Matthew*, 294.
22. *De or.* 24, 2, PG 11, 492C–D.

fore results from being in accord with the divine actions of God. Theodore of Mopsuestia writes, "As when we do ungodly works we give rise to blasphemy (by others), because all the outsiders who see us doing these ungodly works will say about us that we are unworthy to be children of God—so also when we do good works we corroborate the fact that we are children of God, worthy of the freedom of our Father, and show that we have been well educated and that we are living a life worthy of our Father."[23]

Hallowing the Name

The Fathers consistently teach that we make God's name holy through imitation of the divine. God cannot become greater through our praise, but his holiness transforms our persons when we participate in his generous gifts for the world. Peter Chrysologus teaches, "We ask therefore that his name, which is holy in him and through him, be made holy in us. For the name of God is either honored by our act, or blasphemed by our actions."[24] And Jerome echoes this teaching: "'Hallowed be thy name,' not in you but in us. For if the name of God is blasphemed because of sinners among the people, it is, on the contrary, sanctified because of the just."[25] In particular, the pursuit of an ascetical life—a life of prayer and discipline through a separation from sensual vices and an adherence to virtue—allows one to grow in the holy image of God.[26]

Peter Chrysologus makes an important connection between "the name" in the Lord's Prayer and the person of Christ. In

23. Theodore of Mopsuestia, *Commentary on the Lord's Prayer*, trans. Mingana, 8.
24. *Col. serm.* 67.3, CCL 24A, 403, lines 30–31.
25. Jerome of Stridon, *In Mattheum* [*Commentaire sur S. Matthieu I*] I.6.9, ed. Émile Bonnard, SC 242 (Paris: Cerf, 1977), 130, lines 46–48.
26. "We sanctify the name of the Father in grace who is in heaven by mortifying earthly lust, of course, and by purifying ourselves from corrupting passions, since sanctification is the total immobility and mortification of sensual lust"; *Or. dom.*, CCG 23, 43, lines 272–77, in Berthold, *Maximus*, 107.

baptism we become *Christ*-ians and therefore bear the name of Christ. The baptized must treat the name—Christ—as sacred through their imitation of Jesus:

If the name of Christ is sight to the blind, movement for the lame, health for those enervated by various weaknesses, life to the dead, and it sanctifies you yourself—O Man, and the whole of creation, how can you pray for and request the sanctity of his name? Because you have been called a Christian by Christ and therefore you ask that the privilege of so great a name be strengthened by our subsequent merits in you.[27]

Hallowing becomes a mission for the baptized, even the defining activity of the baptized. "But this must be requested by you because you are called Christian by the name of Christ in order that this name be sanctified by your action and honored in you."[28] In the end, this hallowing is the very perfection of the Christian.[29]

The Fathers also encourage the faithful to evangelize through their personal responses to this petition. Imitating God's holiness reveals the divine Glory to the world. Evagrius Ponticus declares, "May thy name be hallowed among us in that, because of our good deeds, we are glorified by the nations who say, 'Behold the true servants of God!'"[30] All nations, all peoples, come to know

---

27. *Col. serm.* 68.4, CCL 24A, 408, lines 63–68. Cyprian also makes a connection between the call to render God's name holy and baptism: "We ask and beseech that we who are made holy in baptism should have the ability to persist in the way we have begun. Our need is of daily sanctification, so that we who daily fail should have our sins purged by continual hallowing"; *De oratione dom.* 12, PL 4, 527A, in Stewart-Sykes, *Lord's Prayer*, 73.

28. *Col. serm.* 69.4, PL 24A, 417, lines 70–73.

29. "The words 'Hallowed be thy name' can also be quite satisfactorily understood in this way—namely, that the hallowing of God is our perfection. And so when we say to him: 'Hallowed be thy name,' we are saying in other words: Make us such, Father, that we may deserve to understand and grasp how great your hallowing is and, of course, that you may appear as hallowed in our spiritual way of life"; *Col.* IX.18.5, PL 49, 791B, in Ramsey, *Conferences*, 342.

30. Evagrius Ponticus, *Our Father*, in *Evagrius Ponticus*, trans. A. M. Casiday (New York: Routledge, 2006), 151.

Christ and the gospel through the light of the living images of God—that is, the saints. "The making of this petition does not imply that the name of God is not holy; it is made so that this name may be held holy by men, that is, so that God may become known to them in such a way that they will deem nothing more holy, nothing which they would be more fearful to offend."[31] Gregory of Nyssa believes that the world will be transformed when all peoples will sanctify the name:

Those who have not yet believed the word of truth closely examine the lives of those who have received the mystery of the faith. If, therefore, people are "faithful" only in name, but contradict this name by their life, whether by committing idolatry for the sake of gain or by disgracing themselves by drunkenness and revelry, being immersed in profligacy like swine in the mud—then the pagans immediately attribute this not to the free choice of these evil-living men, but the mystery which is supposed to teach these things…. Now if this has been properly understood, it will be time to consider the opposite…. Who would be so absurdly unreasonable as not to glorify God if he sees in those who believe in Him a pure life firmly established in virtue?[32]

In effect, the prayer "Hallowed Be Thy Name" encompasses the needs of both the faithful and the searchers, the baptized and the pagans: "Besides this, as regarding our own request, when we say: 'Let your name be hallowed,' we ask that it be hallowed among us who are in him and, at the same time, in others whom the grace of God still awaits, so that we should be obedient to the command to pray for all, even for our enemies" (Mt 5:44).[33]

---

31. *De serm. Dom.* II.5.19, PL 35, 109, lines 411–15, in Kavanagh, *Commentary*, 127.
32. *De or. dom.* 3, GNO 7.2, 35, lines 9–36, in Graef, *Lord's Prayer*, 49.
33. *De oratione* 3, PL 1, 1157A, in Stewart-Sykes, *Lord's Prayer*, 44.

Conclusion: Hallowing the Name Today

Restoring the Sacred

This petition calls for the restoration of the sacredness of God's name. When the name of God becomes simply another word in everyday speech, we empty that name of its transformative power. Furthermore, we fall into the dangerous delusion that we *own* God's name. Past history has demonstrated the deleterious effects in civilizations that have imposed their own images upon the Creator: the invocation of God becomes nothing more than an endorsement of man's vain ambitions. Thus, while nothing can detract from the objective holiness of God, man can distort that holiness in himself and in his culture. Only a restoration of the sacred can liberate man from his self-constructed and perverse fraud.

The Fathers therefore offer an important reminder to the Church in a time of great crisis. Church leaders, ministers, and lay witnesses have lost credibility among the faithful and in the secular sphere because of scandalous behavior and egregious failures in responsibility. They have profaned God's name and, in turn, have driven many away from God. But hallowing heals. A renewed fidelity to God's commandments, as well as a deeper commitment to prayer and Christian living, will glorify God's name and give witness to God's holiness in the world.

The Name as Love and Mission

When the name of God is hallowed, man opens himself to the personal relationship with the One who is Wholly Other. The name of God, "He Who Is," is a gift to man that establishes a radical relationship of love. By treating the name as sacred, man does not attempt to control or distort God's loving action, but rather he gives himself over to God's love. Hans Urs von Balthasar presents this unfathomable condescension of the loving God who shares his name with humanity:

God remains the center and man is related to something outside himself, to the absolute. Man only "has" this love in so far as it "possesses" him, that is to say he does not have it as a possession over which he has control, or which he can point to as one of his powers. Certainly it is not just external to him, but only because *it* seizes hold of him in the innermost depths of his person—*interius intimo meo*. It "organizes" him, not he it; and it makes him—who always struggles against it—into an organ for the performance of its work.[34]

The practice of hallowing God's name therefore allows God—not man—to invest the name with meaning, to surprise man with the infinite depths of his love. The words in the liturgy, the practices of prayer and daily Christian speech that acknowledge the sacredness of God's name shape man's disposition toward divine action; the communal praise of God's name, in all its Glory, unites humanity with the *Trisagion* of the Angels: "Holy, Holy, Holy, Lord God of Hosts!"

The sacredness of God's name also becomes a mission for humanity. An *imitatio Dei* is the Way for the people whom the Divine name possesses. One who is a *Christ*-ian makes that name, the name above all names, sacred in himself. Conformity to the vices of the world—greed, lust, hatred, pride—is blasphemy and idolatry; following the Way gives God glory. Furthermore, the *imitatio Dei* reveals the sacredness of God's name to the World: all nations will hallow God's sacred name when they see its transformative effect in us. "To Him be the power and the glory, forever!"

34. Hans Urs von Balthasar, *Love Alone*, trans. Alexander Dru (New York: Herder and Herder, 1969), 108–9.

5

FOURTH *APORIA*

WAS THERE EVER A TIME WHEN GOD
DID NOT RULE?

> For when is God, in whose hand is the heart of all
> kings (Prov 21:1), not the king?
>
> —Tertullian, *De oratione* 5

Why does Tertullian pose such a question regarding the third petition of the Lord's Prayer? For the North African theologian, the petition "Thy Kingdom Come" seems to request a change in affairs, as if the world were bereft of God's rule and we were now to ask for a divine invasion into occupied territory. The problem, however, is that such an interpretation implies either a weakness in God, since he could not sustain his reign, or God's deliberate abandonment of a broken world—both blasphemous and disturbing propositions. Therefore, with Tertullian, we can now ask: was there ever a time when God did *not* reign over creation?

Tertullian, *De oratione* 5, PL 1, 1158B, in Stewart-Sykes, *Lord's Prayer*, 45.

The Coming of the Kingdom

The twentieth century witnessed fierce scholarly battles for the "Kingdom of God." Albert Schweizer, C. H. Dodd, Joachim Jeremias, J. Dominic Crossan, and John Meier are just some scholars who scrutinized this expression through the lens of modern historical-critical methods.[1] While most scholars would agree that the kingdom was central to Jesus' message, one cannot find a clear consensus regarding its meaning. Is the kingdom something that Jesus and his followers expected to arrive soon? Or is it something that has already begun in the preaching of Jesus? Should it be identified with the liberation and renewal of Israel? With the Church? With the ethical conversion of believers or society? These questions have produced a mass of responses and provoked fierce debates, but clear answers have eluded the practitioners of the historian's craft.

I have no intention of establishing an original position in this historical-critical battlefield. Rather, I will begin with a consideration of the concept of God's reign in the Old Testament, followed by brief discussions of the work of three scholars—N. T. Wright, Gerhard Lohfink, and Pope Benedict XVI—whose insights complement in some ways the trajectory of the Fathers' responses to this chapter's question. This background will allow the Fathers' insights to shine light on the *aporia* of this chapter.

God's Reign in the Old Testament

Jesus' use of the expression "kingdom of God" or, in the Gospel of Matthew, "Kingdom of the Heavens," aroused various associations and reactions in his first-century audience. Dale Patrick

---

1. For summaries of contemporary positions, see N. T. Wright, *Jesus and the Victory of God: Christian Origins and the Question of God* (Minneapolis: Fortress, 1996), 2:220–26; Rudolf Schnackenburg, *God's Rule and Kingdom* (New York: Herder and Herder, 1963), 114–17.

highlights two particular developmental traditions for this potent idea: the universal sovereignty that comes from God's status as the Creator and God's particular sovereignty over the people of Israel.[2] A sampling of examples illustrates these themes:

God's Universal Rule

For dominion belongs to the Lord, and he rules over the nations. (Ps 22: 28)

Yours, O Lord, is the greatness, and the power, and the glory, and the victory, and the majesty; for all that is in the heavens and in the earth is yours; yours is the kingdom. (1 Chr 29:11)

And one [seraph] called to another and said: "Holy, holy, holy is the Lord of hosts; the whole earth is full of his glory." ... And I [Isaiah] said: "Woe is me! For I am lost; for I am a man of unclean lips, and I dwell in the midst of a people of unclean lips; for my eyes have seen the King, the Lord of hosts!" (Is 6: 3; 5)

Yet God my King is from of old, working salvation in the midst of the earth. (Ps 74:12)

God's Rule over Israel

Now therefore, if you will obey my voice and keep my covenant, you shall be my own possession among all peoples; for all the earth is mine, and you shall be to me a kingdom of priests and a holy nation. (Ex 19: 5–6)

Gideon said to them, "I will not rule over you, and my son will not rule over you; the Lord will rule over you." (Jgs 8:23)

And of all my sons (for the Lord has given me many sons) he has chosen Solomon my son to sit upon the throne of the kingdom of the Lord over Israel. (1 Chr 28:5)

2. "The two traditions undoubtedly tended to interact and qualify each other throughout Israelite history and were ripe for synthesis, but it is worth noting that they had not been fully synthesized at the close of the OT canon"; Dale Patrick, "The Kingdom of God in the Old Testament," in *The Kingdom of God in 20th-Century Interpretation*, ed. Wendell Willis (Peabody, Mass.: Hendrickson, 1987), 73.

When Israel went forth from Egypt, the house of Jacob from a people of strange language, Judah became his sanctuary, Israel his dominion. (Ps 114:1–2)

One can also identify passages that point toward a future, or eschatological, reign of God. The suffering of Israel throughout its history—humiliating invasions, occupations, and exile—should have led to the simple dissolution of any distinct identity for the Hebrew people. Yet, the prophetic imagination in particular provided a wellspring of hope for God's "first begotten son." According to the prophets, Israel's travails resulted from its unfaithfulness toward the Covenant, but the restoration of God's rule remained imminent. On the one hand, the arrival of God's reign would include a judgment of the nations: "The clamor will resound to the ends of the earth, for the Lord has an indictment against the nations; he is entering into judgment with all flesh, and the wicked he will put to the sword, says the Lord" (Jer 25:31). On the other hand, this judgment would be both God's and Israel's vindication, the restoration of the exiled son's place before the Creator:

And I will set my glory among the nations; and all the nations shall see my judgment which I have executed, and my hand which I have laid on them. The house of Israel shall know that I am the Lord their God, from that day forward. And the nations shall know that the house of Israel went into captivity for their iniquity, because they dealt so treacherously with me that I hid my face from them and gave them into the hand of their adversaries, and they all fell by the sword. I dealt with them according to their uncleanness and their transgressions, and hid my face from them.

Therefore, thus says the Lord God: Now I will restore the fortunes of Jacob, and have mercy upon the whole house of Israel; and I will be jealous for my holy name.... Then they shall know that I am the Lord their God because I sent them into exile among the nations, and then gathered them into their own Land. (Ez 39:21–25, 28)

This coming of God's reign may also embrace other nations who come to recognize his Glory:

It shall come to pass in the latter days that the mountain of the house of the Lord shall be established as the highest of the mountains, and shall be raised above the hills; and all the nations shall flow to it and many peoples shall come and say: "Come, let us go up to the mountain of the Lord, to the house of the God of Jacob; that he may teach us his ways and that we may walk in his paths." (Is 2:2–3; also see Mi 4:1–4)

The Old Testament therefore contains a variety of themes that will come to the fore both in Jesus' preaching and in the subsequent reflections of the Fathers: the universal and particular rule of God; the seemingly paradoxical ever-present rule of God and the imminent in-breaking of the kingdom; and the joy and peace that come from the kingdom of God.[3]

N. T. Wright: The Kingdom as a New Narrative

N. T. Wright's magisterial, multivolume *Christian Origins and the Question of God* impresses any reader with its scholarship, brilliant analyses, and lucid prose. The second volume, *Jesus and the Victory of God*, examines Jesus' mission and intentions from a historian's perspective. Wright avoids the antitheological—and even anti-Christian—readings of many contemporary scholars, though, as always, the strictly historical approach does sometimes limit the implications of significant texts.[4]

Wright notes that the early Christians understood the kingdom to be both present and future. "The point of the present kingdom is that it is the first-fruits of the future kingdom; and the future kingdom involves the abolition, not of space, time, or

---

3. See Schnackenburg, *God's Rule*, 38.
4. Wright admits this point while examining Jesus' warnings to the people: "Jesus' sayings may have wider implications. That is outside the scope of the present book. But as historians we are bound to read at least the passages discussed in this chapter as warnings about a coming national disaster"; Wright, *Victory*, 323.

the cosmos itself, but rather of that which threatens space, time, and creation, namely, sin and death."[5] For these Christians, the crucified and risen Jesus proved himself to be the central actor of this dramatic new reign through which God the Father was bringing a people home from exile.

Can these themes be rightfully found in Jesus' prophetic ministry? Jesus' teachings on the kingdom can often be cryptic and ambiguous, but they certainly found familiar resonances among his Jewish hearers. What made his words so striking, however, were the ways in which he rewrote the traditional narrative of expectations for the restoration of Israel. Jesus intended his sayings and stories to create a new form of community in which the forgiveness of sins, the renewal of heart, and a commitment to the following of Jesus were all signs of the end of Israel's exile. The time of punishment had terminated, and something new had begun. Jesus invited people to move from one way of being the Israel in expectant exile to another way of being the Israel of the eschatological kingdom.[6] The ministry of Jesus conveyed an invitation, a welcome, a summons, and a challenge to enter the kingdom that his presence and activity had brought to life. "Jesus' retelling of the story [of the kingdom] is not to be squashed down into witty or proverbial aphorisms. It is not to be reduced to timeless moral or doctrinal teaching. He spoke as he acted, as a prophet through whose work YHWH was doing a new thing, indeed *the* new thing for which Israel had waited so long."[7]

The transformative arrival and radical nature of the kingdom can be found in Jesus' resounding summary statements: "The time is fulfilled, and the kingdom of God is at hand; repent, and

5. Wright, *Victory*, 218.

6. In particular, see Wright's explanation of the meaning of "faith." From this perspective, the people come to believe: "(a) This is the moment Israel has been expecting; (b) This moment is constituted and characterized precisely by the presence and activity of Jesus"; Wright, *Victory*, 262–63.

7. Wright, *Victory*, 367.

believe in the gospel" (Mk 1:15); "Repent, for the kingdom of heaven is at hand" (Mt 4:17). Jesus redefines what the kingdom is in the Beatitudes (Mt 5:1–12); in such parables as the sower (Mt 13:1–23) and the mustard seed (Mt 13:31–32); in his invitation to enter the future banquet (Lk 22:28–30); and in many other cryptic stories and images. Repentance and purity of heart demonstrate the presence of the kingdom, while also inspiring others to enter its sphere. The arrival of the kingdom demands a commitment to a new community and way of life in order not to be excluded from its glory: "Not everyone who says to me, 'Lord, Lord,' shall enter the kingdom of heaven, but he who does the will of my Father who is in heaven" (Mt 7:21); "Let the children come to me, and do not hinder them; for to such belongs the kingdom of heaven" (Mt 19:14). But Jesus also points toward a kingdom that will come to fulfillment as the definitive rule of God the Father: "Truly, I say to you, there are some standing here who will not taste death before they see the Son of man coming in his kingdom" (Mt 16:28); "You are those who have continued with me in my trials; as my Father appointed a kingdom for me, so do I appoint for you that you may eat and drink at my table in my kingdom and sit on thrones judging the twelve tribes of Israel" (Lk 22:28–30).

Gerhard Lohfink: Accepting God's Rule

Gerhard Lohfink is a former professor of New Testament at the University of Tübingen and a theologian for the Catholic Integrated Community in Germany. His *Jesus of Nazareth: What He Wanted, Who He Was*, offers an accessible, discriminating presentation of the fruits of contemporary historical scholarship along with reflections upon the pastoral implications of these studies. He begins his book with Jesus' proclamation of the Reign of God as a central theme of the gospel message.

Lohfink particularly highlights the actual presence of the

kingdom, here and now. The summary statement of Mark 1:15—
"The time is fulfilled, and the reign of God has come new;
[therefore] repent, and believe in the good news!"—proclaims
the arrival of the kingdom, not its imminence. God, not man,
has taken the initiative through a definitive entrance into history.
Even repentance "is a consequence of the salvation that is already
present: the time is fulfilled and the reign of God has come near.
At the beginning, then, as throughout the Bible, [it] is God's action, not human action."[8] Lohfink offers no Pelagian reading of
God's reign.

Yet, he does address the expressions of a "future kingdom"
that one finds throughout the gospels. The "not yet" of the kingdom refers to Israel's *response* to the reign initiated by God: "The
people of God, at this moment, has not yet turned back. It is still
in the moment of decision for or against the Gospel. Therefore,
the reign of God is near, but not yet present. It is being offered
to the people of God. It is laid at their feet…. But as long as it is
not accepted it is not near, and the people must still pray: 'Your
kingdom come!'" (Mt 6:10).[9] This acceptance of God's rule, as
accomplished and demonstrated in Jesus, involves sacrifice, even
the taking up of the cross: "What was contained in Jesus' preaching from the very beginning was fully illuminated by his death:
the reign of God demands a change of rulership that human beings must carry out. It demands letting go and self-surrender."[10]

In particular, Lohfink desires to banish what he perceives to
be two misconceptions of the kingdom: its futurity and its indi-
vidualistic realization. The failure to recognize and respond to
the presence of the kingdom strangles its transformative nature:

8. Gerhard Lohfink, *Jesus of Nazareth*: *What He Wanted, Who He Was* (Collegeville, Minn.: Liturgical Press, 2012), 30–31.
9. Lohfink, *Jesus*, 31.
10. Lohfink, *Jesus*, 38.

The explosive power of the reign of God is not only defused by pushing it into the distant future or into a time beyond time. It can also be handed over to impotence by being made homeless. For Jesus the reign of God not only has its own time, it also has its own place in which to be made visible and tangible. That place is the people of God.[11]

The kingdom should not be anticipated, but rather it should be accepted and lived.

Furthermore, the tendency to identify the kingdom as an interior, ethical transformation in the individual's soul feeds into modernity's isolating tendency toward excessive introspection. The reign of God must always be understood with the concept of the *people of God*. This means "the people of God, or the church, is the sacrament of the reign of God in the process of becoming reality."[12]

Pope Benedict XVI: Christ and the Kingdom

In his multivolume work on Jesus, Pope Benedict XVI seeks to liberate Jesus studies from the historical-critical straitjacket in order to "apply new methodological insights that allow us to offer a properly theological interpretation of the Bible."[13] He makes clear his respect for the fruits of contemporary biblical research and often draws upon its insights, but he also applies his bril-

---

11. Lohfink, *Jesus*, 39–40.

12. Lohfink, *Jesus*, 56. Lohfink's presentation can fall into the reduction of the gospel message to a temporal, social gospel. Even his understanding of the Easter appearances is translated into the expectation of opportunities to transform communal life. While such exhortations are laudatory, they fail to capture the radical implications of a world elevated to divine union and they allow for an unintended "ownership" of the kingdom within man's deleterious utopian aspirations. The "not yet" of the kingdom is, in fact, more than just man's refusal to accept and act; it is the expectation of something radically new that can only come from God. See especially the critique of such tendencies in theology in Douglas Farrow, *Ascension and Ecclesia* (Grand Rapids, Mich.: Eerdmans, 1999), 165–254.

13. Benedict XVI, *Jesus of Nazareth: From the Baptism in the Jordan to the Transfiguration* (New York: Doubleday, 2007), xxiii.

liant theological vision to the Word of God. The result is a deeply learned and spiritual reading of essential texts that enriches the life of the Church.

On the one hand, he recognizes the important place that the kingdom holds in the preaching of Jesus: "The Kingdom of God is at hand. A milestone is set up on the flow of time; something new takes place. And an answer to this gift is demanded of man: conversion and faith."[14] Jesus clearly shattered the complacency and false expectation of his world by bringing the message of God's reign.

On the other hand, he laments a contemporary "regnocentrism" that seeks to replace Christ and the Church with a human social gospel. According to proponents of this regnocentrism, the Church mistakenly turned from Jesus' proclamation of the kingdom to Jesus himself, who never intended that he be the content of his preaching. Furthermore, the institution of the Church emerged from this false orientation as a substitute for the genuine promise of the gospel.

This at last, we are told, is the heart of Jesus' message, and it is also the right formula for finally harnessing mankind's positive energies and directing them toward the world's future. "Kingdom," on this interpretation, is simply the name of a world governed by peace, justice and the conservation of creation. This "Kingdom" is said to be the goal of history that has to be attained. This is supposedly the real task of religions: to work together for the coming of the "Kingdom."[15]

The questions therefore center upon the relationship between the kingdom and Christ: Is it wrong to understand Christ as the content of the gospel message? What is Christ's relationship to the kingdom?

In order to respond to these questions, a better definition of the kingdom is required, one that reflects the content of the Scriptures.

14. Benedict XVI, *Jesus*, 47.
15. Benedict XVI, *Jesus*, 54.

We see, then, that the divine lordship, God's dominion over the world and over history, transcends the moment, indeed transcends and reaches beyond the whole of history. Its inner dynamism carries history beyond itself. And yet it is at the same time something belonging absolutely to the present. It is present in the liturgy, in the Temple and synagogue, as anticipation of the next world; it is present as a life-shaping power through the believer's prayer and being: by bearing God's yoke, the believer already receives a share in the world to come.[16]

Thus, though the arrival of the kingdom in the world can already be seen in the lives of believers and the societies transformed by them, it will only reach fulfillment in an unimaginably *new* life from and in God. This kingdom can never be identified with the results of human projects.

In response to the "regno-centrism," Benedict XVI maintains that the kingdom may rightfully be identified with the person of Jesus, thereby making Christ the true focus of the gospel message. "The new proximity of the Kingdom of which Jesus speaks—the distinguishing feature of his message—is to be found in Jesus himself. Through Jesus' presence and action, God has here and now entered actively into history in a wholly new way.... He himself is the treasure; communion with him is the pearl of great price."[17] The kingdom therefore finds its basis in *relationship*—a relationship with Jesus Christ, who is God.

The Fathers and the Kingdom

Defining the Kingdom

How, then, do the Fathers define the kingdom of God? First, the kingdom is established in the liberation of creation from sin and the devil, along with its transfer to the state of grace. When the

16. Benedict XVI, *Jesus*, 57.
17. Benedict XVI, *Jesus*, 61.

devil ceases to reign, God's full dominion will come. This is not to deny that God is always sovereign, but it does indicate that foreign powers—sin and Satan—have been allowed to oppress the world since the fall of humanity. Thus, Peter Chrysologus interprets the petition for the coming of the kingdom as the suppression of invaders and the release of prisoners: "The devil ruled, death ruled and for a long-time mortality was captive. We therefore ask that, since God reigns, the devil may perish, sin may be defeated, death may die and captivity may be captured, in order that we, the liberated, might rule for perpetual life."[18] The advent of the kingdom comes, according to John Cassian, "when the rule of the devil has been cast out of our hearts by the annihilation of the foul vices and God has begun to hold sway in us through the good fragrance of the virtues; when chastity, peace, and humility reign in our minds, and fornication has been conquered, rage overcome, and pride trampled upon."[19]

This divine *Reconquista* possesses a pronounced ethical component that emerges from a deliberate following of Christ. In effect, one must transfer allegiance from the kingdom of Satan to the kingdom that has come in Christ. Origen writes, "But every sinner is tyrannized by the ruler of this present age, since every sinner is claimed by this present wicked age, and yields himself not to the one who 'gave himself for us sinners, to deliver us from this present wicked age,' delivering us 'in accordance with the will of God our Father'" (Gal 1:4).[20] The sinner must therefore give himself over to a new ruler, the person of Jesus Christ.

In turn, Theodore of Mopsuestia preaches that the acceptance of Christ leads to a change in the way one lives even now:

No one who is so placed as to live in the court of a king, and is considered worthy to see him always and converse with him, will go and

18. *Col. serm.* 67.5, PL 24A, 403–4, lines 37–42.
19. *Col.* 9.19, PL 49, 792A, in Ramsey, *Conferences*, 342.
20. *De or.* 25.1, PG 11, 496D–97A, in Stewart-Sykes, *Lord's Prayer*, 169–70.

wander in the bazaars and inns and such like, but will have intercourse only with those who always request the places where he is. In this same way, we who are called to the Kingdom of Heaven, are not allowed to relinquish our fellowship with it or with the things that suit the citizenship therein, and busy ourselves with the commerce of this world in which there is much evil trading and unholy work.[21]

In general, there is a martial spirit in the Fathers' approach to the kingdom: the petition calls one to spiritual combat, aided first and foremost by divine forces that seek to oust the oppressors in the name of Christ. "By this sweet word we obviously offer God this prayer: Let the opposing battle front be broken and the hostile phalanx be destroyed. Bring to an end the war of the flesh against the spirit and let the body no longer harbor the enemy of the soul!"[22]

Second, the Fathers, in a clear contradiction with many contemporary interpreters, do not hesitate to identify the kingdom with persons of the Trinity. Cyprian of Carthage unites the kingdom with the person of Christ, who is both the initiator and fulfillment of God's reign:

It is truly possible, beloved brothers, that Christ himself is the Kingdom of God, whom every day we desire to come and whose arrival we desire to hasten to us soon. For, just as he is our resurrection, because we rise in him, so also he is understood to be the Kingdom of God, because we will reign in him. Thus, we do well to petition for the Kingdom of God, that is, the Kingdom of Heaven, because there is also an earthly kingdom. But whoever has now renounced the present age, that one is greater than its honors and its kingdom. Therefore, whoever dedicates himself to God and Christ, does not desire earthly, but heavenly kingdoms.[23]

Cyprian also links the kingdom to the future coming of Christ and the resurrection of the dead. The kingdom that is Christ

---

21. Theodore of Mopsuestia, *Commentary on the Lord's Prayer*, trans. Mingana, 9.
22. *De or. dom.* 3, GNO 7.2, 39, lines 2–6, in Graef, *Lord's Prayer*, 52.
23. *De oratione dom.* 13, PL 4, 527C–28A.

himself will transform creation through a purely divine initiative: the relationship established between man and Christ will find its fruition in the resurrection from the dead.

Gregory of Nyssa, Evagrius Ponticus, and Maximus the Confessor equate the kingdom with the Holy Spirit. This interpretation is not pure allegory, since Gregory and Maximus cite the authority of a variant reading of the Lord's Prayer in the Gospel of Luke. This alternative reading, which appears in very few sources, replaces "thy Kingdom come" with "let your Holy Spirit come upon us and let it cleanse us."[24] The kingdom therefore arrives in the cleansing from sin that takes place through the Holy Spirit. "'May Thy Holy Spirit come,' he says, 'and purify us.' The proper power and virtue of the Holy Spirit is precisely to cleanse sin; for what is pure and undefiled needs no cleansing.... Therefore the same is the work of either, of the Spirit who cleanses from sin as well as of Christ who has made the purgation."[25] Once again, this interpretation makes the kingdom a divine initiative that suppresses the enemy, sin, and establishes the authentic reign of God. "The kingdom of God is the Holy Spirit; we pray that he will descend upon us."[26]

24. Gregory points directly to Luke as his authority. "Perhaps the same thought is expressed more clearly for us by Luke, who, when he desires the kingdom to come, implores the help of the Holy Spirit. For so he says in his Gospel; instead of *Thy Kingdom come* it reads 'May Thy Holy Spirit come upon us and purify us.' What will the impertinent wordmongers say to these words on the Holy Spirit? By which trick of exegesis will they change the dignity of the kingdom into the lowliness of servitude? For what Luke calls the Holy Spirit, Matthew calls the Kingdom"; *De or. dom.* 3, GNO 7.2, 39, lines 15–40, in Graef, *Lord's Prayer*, 53. For Maximus the Confessor, see *Or. dom.* 4, CCG 23, 41, lines 242–47, in Berthold, *Maximus*, 106.

25. *De or. dom.* 3, GNO 7.2, 40, lines 13–41, in Graef, *Lord's Prayer*, 53. In fact, it is the Trinity that liberates creation from sin: "If therefore the Father forgives sins, the Son takes away the sins of the world, and the Holy Spirit cleanses from the stains of sin those in whom He dwells—what will these fighters against their own life say?," *De or. dom.* 3, GNO 7.2, 44, lines 3–7, in Graef, *Lord's Prayer*, 56.

26. Evagrius Ponticus, *On the Our Father*, in Cassiday, *Evagrius Ponticus*, 151.

Locating the Kingdom

As we have already seen, the Fathers generally emphasize the spiritual and ethical implications of the kingdom. No matter how it is identified, the coming of the kingdom effects the interior transformation of the believer. "May that kingdom come within us and may we be found within that kingdom—that is our petition."[27] Origen, citing a particular understanding of Luke 17:20–21, places the kingdom within the souls of the faithful:

> If, according to the word of our Lord and Savior, the Kingdom of God does not come with observable signs, and people will not say "Here it is!" or "There it is," but the Kingdom of God is within us (Lk 17:20–21), then it is clear that whoever prays for the coming of the Kingdom of God is praying most blessedly for the springing up and the bearing of fruit and the perfection of the Kingdom within himself (for the word is very near, it is in our mouth and in our heart [Dt 30:14]). Moreover, every saint is governed by God and is obedient to the spiritual laws of God who dwells within him as in a well-ordered city. So the Father is present to him, and Christ reigns together with the Father in the soul which has been perfected.[28]

Maximus the Confessor also finds the kingdom within the souls of believers, but he adds a Christological dimension. In order to be a full citizen of the kingdom of God, one must come to resemble God through the growth in virtue. Man, who holds the divine image through his reasoning faculty, becomes the seat of God's reign by conforming himself to the divine likeness: "In it [human reason] the holiness of the divine image has been naturally included to persuade the soul to transform itself by its free will

27. *Serm.* 56.4.6, PL 38, 379, in Kavanagh, *Commentary*, 243.
28. *De or.* 1, PG 11, 496B–C, in Stewart-Sykes, *Lord's Prayer*, 169. Gerhard Lohfink, among others, critiques what he believes to be a misunderstanding of Luke. The Greek *entos hymōn* should not be translated "within you" but "among you" or "in your midst." This understanding gives the kingdom a greater social dimension; see Lohfink, *Jesus*, 50–53.

to the likeness of God."[29] But how can one grow in the divine likeness that one cannot see? By imitation of the true King, Jesus, who reveals the Father:

If the indestructible might of the unfading kingdom is given to the humble and the meek, who would at this point be so deprived of love and desire for the divine gifts as not to tend as much as possible toward humility and meekness to become, to the extent that this is possible for man, the image of God's kingdom by bearing in himself by grace the exact configuration in the Spirit to Christ, who is truly by nature and essence the great King?[30]

The kingdom therefore emerges within the ethical life of believers—individually and collectively (*"Our* Father")—through conformity to the divine likeness in the virtues.

Expecting the Kingdom

When is the kingdom coming? Certainly, the kingdom has already arrived in the person of Jesus Christ, and it becomes a reality in the interior transformation of the faithful. Yet the Fathers also highlight the expectation for something greater, a fulfillment that will come to pass in the future.

This future kingdom will involve judgment. In fact, divine judgment will be the mark of the definitive coming of God's reign. When one prays this petition, one actually asks God to establish justice upon the earth—a frightening proposition in a sinful world. Jerome declared, "At the same time this must be taken into consideration: it takes great audacity and a pure conscience to ask for the kingdom of God, and not to fear judgment."[31] In the divine court the true citizens of the kingdom will become known. Thus, only those who intend to pursue faithful lives should pronounce this petition. "No sinner dares to say this [your kingdom come] or

29. *Or. dom.*, CCG 23, 50, lines 387–89, in Berthold, *Maximus*, 109.
30. *Or. dom.*, CCG 23, 46, lines 334–47, in Berthold, *Maximus*, 108.
31. *In Matt.* I.6.10, SC 242, 130, lines 552–54.

to wish for it, since a person who knows that at his coming he will at once be paid back for his deserts not with a palm or rewards but with punishment has no desire to see the Judge's tribunal."[32]

This expectation of the kingdom in turn gives believers a particular attitude in the world. Every repetition of this petition should lead to an examination of conscience regarding one's attachment to material goods and selfish ambitions. John Chrysostom makes this clear: "Thy Kingdom Come. And this again is the language of a right-minded child, not to be riveted to things that are seen, neither to account things present some great matter; but to hasten unto our Father, and to long for the things to come. And this springs out of a good conscience, and a soul set free from things that are on earth."[33] A Christian is oriented toward the consummation of the kingdom and therefore lives free of excessive temporal anxieties. "But [Christ], who wants us to reach the promised glory of his Kingdom, advises us to long for this in all of our prayers, he wants us to look eagerly toward it with all of our mind."[34] Living for the kingdom requires detachment, longing, and hope during the earthly pilgrimage.

The follower of Christ cannot expect this kingdom to be a mere continuation of this world in a more just or better-organized form. It will be something new and complete. This knowledge brings great consolation and allows one to ask God regularly for the coming reign. "Thy Kingdom come" succinctly gives voice to the deepest desires of the heart. "Therefore, if the open manifestation of the Lord's Kingdom pertains to the will of God and to our expectation, how could anyone ask for an extension of this world, when the Kingdom of God, for whose coming we pray, is directed toward the consummation of this world. We should seek to reign the sooner and not be enslaved the longer."[35]

32. *Col.* 9.19, PL 49, 792B, in Ramsey, *Conferences*, 342.
33. *In Matthaeum* XIX.278, in Prevost, *Matthew*, 294.
34. *Col. serm.* 70.5, CCL 24A, 421, lines 41–44.
35. *De oratione* 5, PL 1, 1159A, in Stewart-Sykes, *Lord's Prayer*, 46.

Conclusion: Calling for the Kingdom of God

God always reigns over creation in his goodness. The petition clearly does not imply that God abandoned the world to its conquerors, nor has God withdrawn to a peaceful seclusion. A world outside of the divine order would return to the *nihil*, the nothing, from which the Father's Word called it forth.

Yet, God also gave angels and men free will either to do his will or to turn toward corrosive selfishness. God respected the free choices of these intelligent beings and allowed opposing powers—Satan, sin, death—to invade his realm. Though these malignant forces cannot annihilate, they can pervert and corrupt. Thus, the petition does in fact beg for a new state of affairs: the ousting of hostile powers and the entrance of God's definitive rule.

There are certain distinct features in the kingdom of God. First, it is a divine, not a human, initiative. This means that the consummation of God's rule can never be equated with a human utopian scheme, no matter how noble the cause. What is to come will be something unprecedented, entirely new. The mystery of Christ's Resurrection and Ascension gives us glimpses of its glory: a creation transformed and made divine. Social justice, political order, world peace, the curing of illnesses, and psychological health do not distinguish the kingdom that is to come. At best, they provide analogies of the joy that will be found in God's reign. But only God can answer what the petition strains to express.

Second, the kingdom will be a trinitarian affair. As the Fathers taught, the Father initiates the arrival of his definitive rule. In turn, the kingdom comes to be in the life and teaching of the incarnate Son. His mission, culminating on the cross, shatters earthly conventions and complacency in order to rewrite humanity's story. The Word enters history and speaks a new way to be, a new hope. Finally, the Holy Spirit effects the kingdom by transforming hearts and minds. The Spirit brings consolation to the deepest groanings of the cosmos.

Third, the kingdom is both *now* and *not yet*. On the one hand the kingdom has already emerged in the presence of Jesus and the action of the Holy Spirit. Christians should feel the joy of this new life today, and they should demonstrate that joy in the way they live. The victory of Christ has established God's rule, and the world should witness God's glory. Yet, on the other hand, *the kingdom has not yet come*. The risen Christ *is not here*; he has ascended to the right hand of the Father, and the consummation of all things will only come in his glorious return. The futurity of the kingdom in the coming of the Lord assures that we now live in a humble and joyful hope.

Finally, the petition calls us to live as genuine citizens of God's realm. The indwelling of the Spirit transforms our vision. We live each moment aware of impending judgment: will Christ recognize us as his own, or as those who chose another ruler—Satan or sin? Citizens of the kingdom are poor in spirit, meek, pure of heart; they see the image of their sovereign in every person, and they treat that image with the love and honor he or she deserves; they feed the hungry, visit the imprisoned, and serve the sick. Every time we pray the Lord's Prayer, we place ourselves before the Creator, reject the falsity of worldly powers, and embrace the truth of God's sovereignty.[36] The world yearns to hear a proclamation of God's kingdom in the Church. "'May your Kingdom come,' because, whether we want it or not, surely it will come. We stir up our desire for this Kingdom in order that it may come to us and we might merit to reign in it."[37]

36. The character of George MacDonald in C. S. Lewis's *The Great Divorce* speaks of the mendacity of Hell and the reality of Heaven: "Hell is a state of mind—ye never said a truer word. And every state of mind, left to itself, every shutting up of the creature within the dungeon of its own mind—is, in the end, Hell. But Heaven is not a state of mind. Heaven is reality itself. All that is fully real is Heavenly"; see Lewis, *The Great Divorce* (New York: Harper Collins, 2001), 70–71.

37. Augustine of Hippo, *Epistula* 130, in *Epistulae*, PL 33, 502, lines 11, 21.

6

FIFTH *APORIA*

Every religion must confront the problem of theodicy. Gottfried Wilhelm Leibnitz (1646–1714) coined this term in order to convey the problem of God's (Greek, *theos*) justice (Greek, *dikē*): How can there be a just and good God in a world plagued by suffering and sin?[1] In fact, one might argue that theodicy poses *the* question for believers and that the quality of the response becomes a measure of truth for every presentation of theism.

Many people have abandoned their faith before this seemingly irresolvable paradox. Since there is suffering in the world, either God is not good or God is not omnipotent—which essentially means God is not God. If God possesses even a partially corrupt or limited will, he cannot truly be divine. He is at best a superior creature, no more. Thus, many reject the existence of God and prefer the more "rational" acceptance of an indifferent cosmos spiraling toward inevitable destruction.

The third petition in the Lord's Prayer therefore poses a ques-

---

1. Gottfried Wilhelm von Leibniz, *Theodicy: Essays on the Goodness of God, the Freedom of Man, and the Origin of Evil*, ed. Austin Farrer, trans. E. M. Huggard (London: Routledge, 1952).

tion that falls within the purview of theodicy: Are there limits to the divine will? Augustine formulates the question in this way: "Shall God not accomplish His will unless you make that petition?... If He is almighty, why do you pray that His will be done?"[2] The fact that we must *ask* for the fulfillment of the divine will implies either that God's will can be frustrated or that God perversely plays with the world. Why must we beg for the accomplishment of God's plan?

Preliminary Considerations

The Position of the Petition in the Lord's Prayer

Since this petition only appears in Matthew's Gospel, some scholars deem it a coda that explicates the content of the coming kingdom. Thus, R. T. France believes that "the essence of the coming of God's kingship is that he is duly obeyed and his purpose fulfilled."[3] The petition therefore both acknowledges the goodness of the divine will—the request confirms that God's will is good for creation—and asks that human beings conform themselves to the divine plan and precepts. God's kingdom manifests itself in the active conformity of persons with God's will.

Yet, does this petition refer to what *God* does or to what *man* does? Does it pray that God will impose his will upon human beings and make them active participants, or does it ask that human beings submit their freedom to the divine will? Biblical scholar Ulrich Luz sees both of these desires expressed in the single petition: "When Jesus prays 'let your will be done,' he is not only asking God to do whatever he wants to do; at the same time he is also asking for the power to associate actively with this will of

---

2. *Serm.* 56.7, PL 38, lines 379–80, in Kavanagh, *Commentary*, 244.
3. R. T. France, *The Gospel of Matthew* (Grand Rapids, Mich.: Eerdmans, 2007), 247.

God."[4] Human beings must actively ally themselves with the divine will through the effective appropriation of the law and the imitation of the Son, but they cannot fulfill this mission without divine assistance. "Those who long for God's will on earth in the future should live consistently with that longing in the present, working for God's righteousness and seeking his will here."[5]

Furthermore, some scholars link this petition to the words "on earth as it is in heaven." As we noted in chapter 3, the singular "heaven" in combination with "earth" generally refers to the entirety of creation—both the earthly realm and the place of the angelic hosts. The distinction between the two realms can also imply the need for the two created divisions to become one in divine praise: one prays for "a perfect harmony between the way in which heaven and earth run."[6] Active participation on the part of humans will therefore form a united kingdom. "In this petition, we pray that everyone on earth join the angels and saints in serving the king, revering his holy name, and doing his will perfectly—just as it is done in heaven."[7]

The Obedience of Jesus

"Jesus himself provides the example of obedience."[8] Throughout the Gospel of Matthew, Jesus both speaks of the fulfillment of the Father's will and demonstrates the fulfillment in himself. In fact, Jesus fully identifies himself with the Father's will:

At that time Jesus declared, "I thank you, Father, Lord of heaven and earth, that you have hidden these things from the wise and understand-

4. Ulrich Luz, *Matthew 1–7: A Commentary* (Minneapolis: Fortress, 2007), 318.

5. Craig Keener, *A Commentary on the Gospel of Matthew* (Grand Rapids, Mich.: Eerdmans, 1999), 220.

6. Harrington, *Matthew*, 95. Also see Lohmeyer, *Lord's Prayer*, 114.

7. Curtis Mitch and Edward Sri, *The Gospel of Matthew* (Grand Rapids, Mich.: Baker Academic, 2010), 106.

8. Robert Gundry, *Matthew: A Commentary on His Handbook for a Mixed Church under Persecution* (Grand Rapids, Mich.: Eerdmans, 1994), 106.

ing and revealed them to infants; yes, Father, for such was your good will (*eudokia*). All things have been delivered to me by my Father; and no one knows the Son except the Father and no one knows the Father except the Son and any one to whom the Son chooses to reveal him." (Mt 11: 25–27)

In this passage Jesus invokes the Father, whose loving plan embraces the entire cosmos—heaven and earth. Jesus reveals the Father's will to those who remain open to his message: the *nēpioi*, the infants or the "non-speakers," who remain outside the circles of the wise and learned.[9] Furthermore, the Father's will is *good* and works for the life of even the least of humanity: "Thus it is not the will (Greek: *thelēma*) before your Father in the Heavens that one of these little ones perish" (Mt 18:14). Obedience to God's will therefore liberates one from anxiety in the world, since God's plan works for salvation:

Therefore do not be anxious saying, "What shall we eat?" or "What shall we drink?" or "What shall we wear?" For the Gentiles seek all these things; and your heavenly Father knows that you need them all. But seek first his kingdom and his righteousness, and all these things shall be yours as well." (Mt 6:31–33)

The Father desires first and foremost that man invest his life with righteousness, as defined by the law and the teacher, Jesus Christ. "Not every one who says to me, 'Lord, Lord,' shall enter the kingdom of heaven, but he who does the will of my Father who is in heaven" (Mt 7:21).

One important scene that illustrates Jesus' obedience is his struggle at Gethsemane, at the start of his Passion. It has long been noted that his words in the dialogue with the Father match the petition in the Lord's Prayer: "My Father, if it be possible, let this chalice pass from me; nevertheless, not as I will, but as you

---

9. See Harrington, *Matthew*, 167.

will" (Mt 26:39).[10] This moving scene, which will be reviewed from the ancients' perspective in the following section, reveals the cost of conforming to the Father's will in a broken world. The Father's will is ultimately for man's good, but this does not exempt one—not even Jesus—from facing the violent forces that oppose it. Jesus looks past the approaching storm and draws upon his absolute trust in the Father. His obedience overcomes all fear and revulsion to accept the chalice of suffering. Right up to the end Jesus does not seek his own will, but the will of the one who sent him (Mt 5:30).

The connection between the Father's will and its fulfillment in Jesus is found elsewhere in the Scriptures. In the Gospel of John, Jesus makes the content of the Father's will clear:

For I have come down from heaven, not to do my own will, but the will of him who sent me; and this is the will of him who sent me, that I should lose nothing of all that he has given me, but raise it up at the last day. For this is the will of my Father, that everyone who sees the Son and believes in him should have eternal life; and I will raise him up on the last day. (Jn 6:38–40)

The completion of the divine plan will take place in Jesus. In particular, the consummation of all things is the resurrection, which will embrace all who have faith in him.

The Pauline Epistles speak of Jesus' obedience to the Father and fulfillment of the divine will through his death upon the cross. In the Letter to the Galatians, Paul greets the community,

10. The versions of Mark and Luke differ slightly from Matthew's version: "Abba, Father, all things are possible to you; remove this chalice from me; yet not what I will, but what you will" (Mk 14:36); "Father, if you are willing, remove this chalice from me; nevertheless not my will, but yours, be done" (Lk 22:42). Thus, Matthew's version is much closer to the wording of the version of the prayer that he transmits in his own Gospel; see Lohmeyer, *Lord's Prayer*, 115; Harrington, *Matthew*, 373.

saying, "Grace to you and peace from God the Father and our Lord Jesus Christ, who gave himself for our sins to deliver us from the present evil age, according to the will (*thelēma*) of God our Father" (Gal 1:3–4). The hymn at the beginning of the Letter to the Philippians emphasizes Jesus' humble obedience to the Father's will by handing over his life:

Let each of you look not only to his own interests, but also to the interests of others. Have this mind among yourselves, which was in Christ Jesus who, *though he was in the form of God, did not count equality with God a thing to be grasped, but emptied himself, taking the form of a servant, being born in the likeness of men. And being found in human form he humbled himself and became obedient unto death, even death on a cross. Therefore God has highly exalted him and bestowed on him the name which is above every name, that at the name of Jesus every knee should bow, in heaven and on earth and under the earth, and every tongue confess that Jesus Christ is Lord, to the glory of God the Father.* (Phil 2:5–11)[11]

On the one hand, this passage also describes Christ's obedience as that which effects his glory and reveals the glory of the Father. The hymn echoes the humble submission of Jesus in Gethsemane when he accepted the chalice of suffering. On the other hand, the context of the hymn makes Jesus' obedience an example: the community should not promote its own interests and ambitions, but it should imitate the humble obedience of Jesus for the sake of others. As Christ emptied himself in the name of the Father, so must they humble themselves as Christ's followers.

11. For some, these passages seem to suggest that the Father *willed* the crucifixion of Jesus—a problematic notion that seems to make God desire evil. Nicholas Lombardo, OP, offers an overview of the problem from both philosophical and theological perspectives and provides some important insights regarding intentionality and unintended effects; see Lombardo, *The Father's Will: Christ's Crucifixion and the Goodness of God* (Oxford: Oxford University Press, 2013).

The Fathers Seek God's Will

Equality with the Angels

The coda "on earth as it is in heaven" shapes the Fathers' interpretation of this petition, since it implies a fracture—the split between the earthly world and the realm of the angels—that must be healed through the unifying power of the will. The human will either severs earth from heaven through sin or establishes communion with heaven through loving obedience to God. All things become one in God only when creatures endowed with free will—men and angels—share in the goodness of divine volition. Peter Chrysologus preaches, "This is the kingdom of God, when in heaven and on earth there is the will of God alone, when God is mind in all men, when God lives, when God acts, when God reigns, when God is all, in order that, according to the words of the Apostle, God may be 'all things in all' of us."[12]

The communion between heaven and earth emerges from the equality between men and angels. The ideal of becoming *isangelos*, equal to an angel, held an important place in early Christian ascetical practices.[13] The inspiration for this concept came from the Scriptures, when Jesus, responding to the Sadducees' question regarding the resurrection, said, "For they cannot die anymore, because they are equal to angels (*isangeloi*), being sons of the resurrection" (Lk 20:36). Jesus teaches that marriage and other temporal relationships do not apply to the resurrected because they have entered into an entirely different mode of existence that resembles that of the heavenly host: equality with the angels.

On this basis, many ancient ascetics described spiritual progress as an ascent toward the angelic state. A purification of the mind and spirit, along with a separation from disordered mate-

---

12. *Col. serm.* 67.6, CCL 24A, 404, lines 43–47.
13. From the Greek world *askēsis*, exercise. The monks in the desert were particularly noted for their rigorous spiritual exercises and submission to God.

rial desires, brings one ever closer to the angelic likeness. Equality with the angels establishes a spiritual stability that permeates the Christian and renders him a denizen of heaven even while he lives on earth. Clement of Alexandria, in the second century, described this human ascent to the angels:

The conversion that struggles to the point of love even now establishes the knowing subject as a friend to that which is known. And such a one, perhaps in anticipation, acquires equality with the angel (*to isangelos einai*). Indeed, after the highest fulfillment in the flesh, he transforms himself continually, as is proper, into that which is better. He rushes forward through the holy *hebdomad* [the heavens, the seven planets] into the Father's hall, the Lord's dwelling. He will be, so to speak, a stable light and will remain, in his particular way, entirely and in every part immutable.[14]

This spiritual ideal could sometimes lead to excessive practices, as in the case of the ascetic John Kolobos, who, convinced he had reached the angelic state, stopped eating and drinking—at least until extreme hunger convinced him of his folly.[15] Yet, the early monks and ascetics generally limited the concept to such things as frugality, fasting, abstinence, communal harmony, and prayer—all things that make one more spiritual, stable, and less dependent upon the deceptive vicissitudes of material existence.[16] They sought the heavenly state of existence, a life free of evil and oriented fully to God.[17]

---

14. Clement of Alexandria, *Stromateis* VII.10.57, in *Stromate VII*, ed. Alain le Boulluec, SC 428 (Paris: Cerf, 1997), 186–88. Also see Origen of Alexandria, *Contra Celsum* 4.29, in *Contre Celse II*, ed. Marcel Borret, SJ, SC 136 (Paris: Cerf, 1968), 252.

15. See *Apophthegmata patrum*, PG 65, 204C–D.

16. For instance, see Gregory of Nyssa, *De hominis opificio*, PG 44, 189A; Gregory of Nyssa, *De virginibus*, ed. J. P. Cavaronos, GNO 8 (Leiden: Brill, 1952), 309; Macarius of Egypt, *Homilia* 3.1, PG 34, 468C.

17. For a fuller treatment of this theme see John Gavin, SJ, *"They Are Like the Angels in the Heavens": Angelology and Anthropology in the Thought of Maximus the Confessor* (Rome: Studia Ephemeridis Augustinianum, 2009), 189–225.

The angels obey the divine will perfectly and thereby unify themselves fully with God; in turn, human beings, by imitating the angelic state as much as possible, make themselves co-citizens of heaven. John Cassian writes, "There cannot be a greater prayer than to desire that earthly things should deserve to be equal to heavenly ones. For what does it mean to say: 'Thy will be done on earth as it is in heaven,' if not that human beings should be like angels and that, just as God's will is fulfilled by them in heaven, so also all those who are on earth should do not their own but his will?"[18] Human beings must therefore overcome their pride and submit to the humble service of their Creator. "'May your will be done in heaven and on earth,' in order that in that way that the angels serve you faultlessly in the heavens, so may men serve you on earth."[19] Angels and men may be different species, but they are both servants blessed by the same, unified mission: the eternal praising of God. "Blessed that day which joins, associates and equates the wills of earthly beings with celestial beings, in order that one and the same will be among dissimilar substances."[20]

Man's earthly life offers due worship to God when he freely directs himself toward God as the fulfillment of all desires. "Thus indeed we will be found to be giving God worship in every way in imitation of the angels in heaven, and we shall exhibit on earth the same manner of life as the angels in having as they do the mind totally moved in the direction of nothing less than God."[21] The human will honors God when it chooses Good over Evil in company with the celestial hierarchy: "In other words: As thy will is done by the thrones and principalities and powers and dominations and all the supramundane hosts, where no evil hinders the action of the good, so may the good be accomplished also in

---

18. *Col.* IX.20, PL 49, 792B–93A, in Ramsey, *Conferences*, 342.
19. *In Matt.* 6.10, SC 242, 130, lines 55–57.
20. *Col. serm.* 68.6, PL 24A, 409, lines 77–79.
21. *Or. dom.*, CCG 23, 58–59, lines 545–49, in Berthold, *Maximus*, 113.

us."[22] This petition therefore encourages man to strive for this ideal even now, to unite heaven and earth through conformity to the divine will in imitation of the angels. St. John Chrysostom tells his flock, "For there is nothing to hinder our reaching the perfection of the powers above, because we inhabit the earth; but it is possible even while abiding here, to do all, as though already placed on high."[23]

Reforming the Will

Sin deformed the human will and infected it with disordered desires. Though the will naturally directs even fallen man toward that which fulfills his nature, nonetheless sin clouds the intellect regarding that which is truly Good. Gregory of Nyssa summarizes this teaching:

Now the holy Apostle counsels us in one of his letters to *be zealous for the better gifts* (1 Cor 12:31). It is our aim not that we should be persuaded to desire the things that are good; (for to incline towards the good is one of the inherent characteristics of human nature)—but that we should not be mistaken in our judgment as to what is good. It is here that our life is most subject to error, that we cannot clearly distinguish what is good by nature and what is mistakenly supposed to be such.[24]

The will and intellect must be re-formed through cooperation with divine action. The petition of the Lord's Prayer therefore asks God for guidance and aid that human beings might desire genuine and fulfilling goods. St. Augustine explains the nature of this divine synergy:

That the will of God be done in you is one thing; that it be done *by you* is another thing. For no other reason, therefore, but that it may be well for you, do you pray that God's will be done in you, for, whether it be well or ill with you, it shall be done in you. But may it be done also

---

22. *De or. dom.* 4, GNO 7.2, 50, lines 15–20, in Graef, *Lord's Prayer*, 62.

23. *In Matthaeum* XIX.279, in Prevost, *Matthew*, 295.

24. *Beat.* 5, GNO 7.2, 125, lines 6–14, in Graef, *Lord's Prayer*, 131.

by you.... Never is anything done by you except what He does in you. Sometimes, indeed, He does in you what is not done by you. But never is anything done by you, unless He does it in you.[25]

The drama of the will plays out in the war between the flesh, clouded by sin, and the spirit, enlightened by God. Some Fathers interpret "earth" as the flesh and "heaven" as the spirit and thereby emphasize the importance to unite these divisions through the proper exercise of the will: "heaven," the spirit, and "earth," the flesh, must harmonize in their shared desire for the Good. Tertullian, for example, considers the petition to be a call for the reintegration of the human person: "For, by a figurative interpretation of flesh and spirit, the heaven and the earth indicate ourselves."[26] Cyprian preaches the need for this personal unity: "For there is strife between the flesh and the spirit, a daily contest as they clash with one another so that we do not the things we desire ... and therefore we ask that reconciliation be brought about between the two through the help and assistance of God, and so, while the will of God is undertaken both in the spirit and in the flesh, the soul which is reborn through him may be saved."[27]

The properly ordered will forms man in the divine likeness and gives him a new mode of existence even while continuing to live in the world. In effect, the Christian receives liberation from disordered attractions and seeks God above all things. "We should only consider as unqualified good that which is pleasing to God, and endeavor in everything to spurn the pleasures of this world. We should also bear the tribulations that befall us, place the will of God before everything, and consider ourselves happy

---

25. *Serm.* 56.5, PL 38, 380, in Kavanagh, *Commentary*, 244–45. Gregory of Nyssa shares this teaching: "Because Thy will is temperance, but I am carnal and sold under sin, may this good Will be accomplished, in me by Thy power; and so it is also with justice, piety, and deliverance from the passions"; *De or dom.* 4, GNO 7.2, 48, lines 3–13, in Graef, *Lord's Prayer*, 60.

26. *De oratione* 4, PL 1, 1157B, in Stewart-Sykes, *Lord's Prayer*, 45.

27. *De oratione Dom.* 16, PL 4, 529C–30C, in Stewart-Sykes, *Lord's Prayer*, 76.

when we act thus, even if all the afflictions of this world should surround us."[28] "To be pleasing to God" restores man's vision of the Good and conforms him to the will of God. The properly ordered will also transforms man's fundamental community, the Church. St. Augustine directs his audience to seek a single will in the bridegroom, Christ, and the bride, the Church: "It would be as though we were to pray that the Father's will be accomplished in the woman who is espoused to the Son, just as it is accomplished in the Son who fulfilled the Father's will—for heaven and earth are aptly taken as husband and wife, since the earth is fruitful because the heavens make it fertile."[29] God's will, though performed in the individual, in fact constitutes the communion that is the Church of Christ.

Jesus' Cup

As we saw in the first section of this chapter, the Scriptures point toward Jesus as the model of obedience to the Father. Matthew, in particular, makes a clear connection between this petition from the Lord's Prayer and Jesus' prayer in Gethsemane: "My Father, if it be possible, let this chalice pass from me; nevertheless, not as I will, but as you will" (Mt 26:39). The Fathers did not fail to pick up on this allusion and focused upon the scene of Christ's suffering as a demonstration of perfect obedience to the Father. The Master writes:

Our Lord and Savior shows us this holy will by giving us the example of its being done in himself in order to suppress the free will of the flesh in us when he says: "I have come not to do my own will, but to do the will of the one who sent me." And again he says in his holy passion: "My Father, if it is possible, let this cup pass me by." ... Then follows: "If

28. Theodore of Mopsuestia, *Commentary on the Lord's Prayer*, trans. Mingana, 10.
29. *De serm. Dom.* II.6.24, CCL 35, 113, lines 513–14, in Graef, *Lord's Prayer*, 131–32.

this cup cannot pass by without my drinking it, your will be done." See therefore that whatever we choose by our own will is patently unjust, and whatever is justly imposed on us against our will by the one who has command over us is accounted to our credit.[30]

Tertullian asks his audience to imitate Christ's self-emptying response: "The Lord likewise, when he desired to demonstrate in his own flesh the weakness of the flesh through the suffering of the passion, said: 'Father, take away this cup.' And, recollecting himself: 'Nonetheless, let not my will but yours be done' (Mt 26:39). He was himself the will and power of the Father, and yet, in order to show the endurance that is due, he abandoned himself to the Father's will."[31] Origen notes that Christ, through "his obedience even to death" (Phil 2:8), united heaven and earth—that is, he united his divine and human natures in a perfect act of submission to the Father: "For the man who is in the Savior receives authority over whatever is in heaven, which is the proper domain of the only-begotten one, so that the communion between them might be perfected. For this humanity is mingled and united with his divinity."[32]

Maximus the Confessor, in particular, understands Christ's obedience in Gethsemane as the redirection of disobedient humanity's freedom. In his later years Maximus became involved in the Monothelite controversy, which emerged from the question of whether Christ had both a divine will and human will (*thelēma*) after the incarnation—the *dyothelite*, or two-will position—or a single divine will after the incarnation—a *monothelite*, or one-will position.[33] For Maximus, the denial of two wills in Christ effectively denied his full humanity and failed to

---

30. *Regula*, SC 105, 306–8, lines 114–34, in Eberle, *Rule*, 97–98.

31. *De oratione* 4, PL 1, 1158, in Stewart-Sykes, *Lord's Prayer*, 45.

32. *De or.* 26.4, PG 11, 501D, in Stewart-Sykes, *Lord's Prayer*, 173.

33. For a concise history of the Monothelite controversy, see Demetrios Bathrellos, *The Byzantine Christ: Person, Nature, and Will in the Christology of Saint Maximus the Confessor* (Oxford: Oxford University Press, 2004), 60–98.

understand the importance of Christ's transformation of the human will in himself. In Gethsemane and in his passion,[34] Christ re-formed humanity's will by conforming it with his divine will. His apparent conflict in the scriptural scene in fact reveals that the person of Christ freely willed in a divine-human manner to accept the suffering and the complete abandonment to the Father on the Cross. Thus, in the words of Robert Louis Wilken, Christ's human will "is not less human, but more human because it is in harmony with the divine will."[35]

Through the incarnation, the Son of God divinized his human will—he rendered it divine—and restored man's freedom to give himself fully to God's transforming grace. Christ "naturally moved and stamped (Greek: *typein*) the will both as his own and as natural for his soul. He fulfilled, in a real way, the great mystery of God's plan for us."[36] In Gethsemane, Jesus made his human will a type (*typos*) of his divine will, giving it a new form and liberating it from slavery to disordered attractions. Thus, the Father's will was accomplished in the Son, but that accomplishment now opens the way for man to conform himself in obedience to the Father.

Conclusion: Your Will Be Done

According to the Fathers, this *aporia* can only be understood in the context of freedom: God's freedom, the angels' freedom, and the freedom of men. The urgency of asking that "God's will be

34. On the importance of this scene in the Monothelite controversy and the scholarly debates surrounding modern interpretations see Bathrellos, *Byzantine Christ*, 140–47; M. Doucet, "La volonté humaine du Christ, spécialement en son agonie: Maxime le Confesseur interprète de l'Écriture," *Science et Esprit* 37 (1985): 136–41; F. M. Léthel, *Théologie de l'agonie du Christ* (Paris: Éditions Beauchesne, 1996).

35. Wilken, *Early Christian Thought*, 131; Jonathan Bieler, "Maximus the Confessor on Christ's Human Will," in *Communio* 43, no. 1 (Spring 2016): 58–66.

36. Maximus the Confessor, *Opuscula theologica et polemica* 1, PG 91, 32A. On the remodeling of the will see Gavin, *"They Are Like Angels,"* 246–49.

done" becomes evident when reflecting upon the drama of freedom in a cosmos of intelligent creatures endowed with free will.

The triune God freely elected to create beings—angels and men—with the freedom to choose. This was a humiliating act, since God not only made creatures in his likeness, he also allowed them the possibility of refusing his deifying grace. Men and angels, created to glorify the Creator, could also reject the very mission that would fulfill their deepest desires. In short, God humbly made beings who could either freely love him … or spurn his love. Why some angels chose irrationality and evil remains a mystery; why man sought to become a god on his own terms remains an inexplicable folly. Yet, God freely allowed them to make their choices and assume the consequences. To abrogate their freedom, to ignore their responsibility, would be *to unmake them*: they would cease to be free, rational beings and become, at best, irrational beasts.

The angels, those spirits who obeyed the divine will, reveal the true nature of heaven. Heaven is not so much a place as the state of being in loving conformity with God. The celestial host freely participates in divine stability and happiness, effectively bringing heaven into existence. In fact, the very name "angel"—from the Greek *angelos*, "an announcer" or "a messenger"—designates the mission that orients their being: they live to conform themselves to the divine Word and to proclaim that Word to all.

Human beings, because they are creatures of body and spirit, find themselves still within the struggle to fulfill their nature by conforming themselves to the divine likeness. Their fallen wills, as Gregory of Nyssa noted, are more easily inclined toward evil than toward good: "Therefore if we feel an impulse to do evil we need no help; for evil accomplishes itself in our will. But if there is an inclination towards something good, we need God to carry the desire into effect."[37] If human beings are to enter heaven—the

37. *De or. dom.* 4, GNO 7.2, 48, lines 3–7, in Graef, *Lord's Prayer*, 60.

free, graced participation in the divine life—their will must be re-constituted by God in a manner that does not "unmake them"—that is, in a manner that does not abrogate their freedom.

Thus, the Father sent his Only Begotten Son. God became man in order that man might become divine. Yet this also required a re-formation of man's will through a radical break from disordered attractions and a total abandonment in love to the Father's good will. Jesus conformed his human will with his divine will—"My Father, if it be possible, let this chalice pass from me; nevertheless, not as I will, but as you will"—and gave himself freely and completely to the Father on the cross. He became both the cause and model of humanity's hope: to become heaven through obedience to the Father.

The question of theodicy, posed at the beginning of this chapter, therefore finds its response not in a tight, explanatory formula, but in a mystery—the mystery of freedom exhibited most fully upon the cross. "Thy will be done" means joining the Son in his obedience to the Father and taking up the cross.

For this reason the Father loves me, because I lay down my life, that I may take it again. No one takes it from me, but I lay down of my own accord. I have the power to lay it down, and I have the power to take it again; this charge I have received from my Father. (Jn 10:17–18)

God does not allow death to have the final word, but instead removes its sting. In Christ, the Father's will is done, uniting heaven and earth in his love; now man prays that his will may also join the Son upon the tree through a grace-filled obedience to the will of the Father.

7

SIXTH *APORIA*

WHY SHOULD WE SEEK BREAD?

"Give us this day our daily bread." The first of the "we petitions"—the four petitions that voice *our* needs to God—has inspired many debates over the centuries. The grammatical structure, word choices, ambiguous context, and other matters have puzzled the Fathers and modern exegetes alike. Yet, as in all of the *aporiai* in the Lord's Prayer, great fruit comes to those who labor in this field.

One question in particular regarding this petition comes to the fore: What, exactly, is the *object* of this request? Is it actual bread? Or is bread a symbol for something spiritual? This question becomes more pronounced, given that the petition appears to contradict Jesus' own teaching. Maximus the Confessor explains:

The Savior has led me to this understanding of the present word when he expressly enjoins his disciples not to be overly concerned with sensible food. "Do not worry" he says, "about your life, what you will eat or what you will drink; nor for your bodies, what you will wear. For all these things the people of the world worry about. But seek first the kingdom of God and his justice, and all of this will be given to you in abundance." *How then does he teach us to pray for what he had previously ordered us not to seek after?*[1]

Indeed, this request stands out in the prayer as something mundane and trivial. The other petitions for forgiveness, aid against temptation, and liberation from evil involve the very salvation of our souls, while the desire for bread only contributes to the passing needs of the body. Why would Jesus, who commands his followers to focus on things of the spirit, tell us to request bread from the Father?

Some Problems in the Text

The Two Versions of the Petition

Matthew's version of the prayer differs in some significant ways from Luke's. First, though both Greek verbs for "give" are imperatives, they differ in tense. Matthew has a Greek aorist imperative, which indicates a complete and one-time action: "Give us *once and for all* our bread." Luke, however, has a present imperative, implying repeated action: "Give us bread *regularly.*" For some commentators, Matthew's selection indicates the eschatological import of the petition—that is, we ask for something to be given *definitively* to us at the end of history; but Luke's implies the desire for the satisfaction of regular, basic needs in life.[2]

Second, Matthew's version contains the word *sēmeron*, which is generally translated as "today." Thus, we are told to pray for the fulfillment to come now, on this day. Luke, however, uses the expression *to kath'hēmeran*, which means "daily" or "each day." In keeping with the tense of the verb, Luke's version asks for bread

---

1. *Or. dom.*, CCG 23, 60, lines 571–80, in Berthold, *Maximus*, 113–14.
2. Matthew's "one time only" request therefore fits Jesus' basic teaching from later in the chapter: "Therefore do not be anxious about tomorrow, for tomorrow will be anxious for itself" (Mt 6:34); see Carmignac, *Recherches*, 120.

to be bestowed regularly, every day.[3] To flush out some of the implications of these distinctions in tenses and expressions, we need to examine two other words that appear in both texts.

The Meaning of "Bread" in the Scriptures

Contemporaries of Jesus would have detected many levels of meaning and significant allusions in the simple word "bread." In the Greco-Roman world bread was associated with civilization and sustenance, as well as with such religious concepts as immortality and resurrection.[4] For a Jewish audience, however, the word "bread" recalled significant passages from the Scriptures. It reminded them of the love that God demonstrated in their exodus from slavery to the Egyptians, which the people commemorated yearly: "Seven days you shall eat unleavened bread, and on the seventh day there shall be a feast to the Lord.... And you shall tell your son on that day, 'It is because of what the Lord did for me when I came out of Egypt'" (Ex 13:6, 8). God also fed them during their wanderings in the desert with the gift of *manna*, the bread that came with the dew of the morning (Ex 16). Passages also compare the nourishing qualities of bread with the even greater sustenance found in the word or wisdom of God.

And he [God] humbled you and let you hunger and fed you with manna, which you did not know, nor did your fathers know; that he might make you know that man does not live by bread alone, but that man lives by everything that proceeds out of the mouth of the Lord. (Dt 8:3)

"Behold the days are coming," says the Lord God, "when I will send a famine on the land; not a famine of bread, nor a thirst for water, but of hearing the words of the Lord." (Am 8:11)

Wisdom has built her house, she has set up her seven pillars. She has slaughtered her beasts, she has mixed her wine, she has also set her

3. See Raymond Brown, "*Pater Noster*," 194–95.
4. Michael Joseph Brown, "'*Panem Nostrum*': The Problem of Petition and the Lord's Prayer," *Journal of Religion* 80, no. 4 (2000): 602–3.

table. She has sent out her maids to call from the highest places in the town, "Whoever is simple, let him turn in here!" To him who is without sense she says, "Come eat of my bread and drink of the wine I have mixed. Leave simpleness, and live, and walk in the way of insight." (Prv 9:1–6)

Bread, the basic substance of life, therefore came from a God who cared for his people, but, at the same time, it pointed toward that higher spiritual nourishment that formed Israel as the Chosen People. The simple word suggests divine attention to bodily needs, as well as spiritual and intellectual formation through divine gift.[5]

The New Testament offers a significant nexus of events and teachings that shape the interpretation of "bread." In particular, Jesus' multiplication of the loaves revealed not only God's continuing *philanthropia*, or love for humanity, but also Jesus' identity as a new Moses who provides the *manna* to the people (Mk 6:31–44, 8:1–9; Mt 14:13–21, 15:32–39; Lk 9:12–17; Jn 6:1–14). More importantly, Jesus recasts the Passover meal as a commemoration of his impending death, making the bread and wine into the signs of the breaking of his flesh and the shedding of his blood:

Now as they were eating, Jesus took bread, and blessed, and broke it, and gave it to the disciples and said, "Take, eat; this is my body." And he took a chalice, and when he had given thanks he gave it to them, saying, "Drink of it, all of you; for this is my blood of the covenant, which is poured out for many for the forgiveness of sins. I tell you I shall not drink again of this fruit of the vine until that day when I drink it new with you in my Father's kingdom." (Mt 26:26–29; also see Lk 22:14–23; Mk 14:22–25)

The Gospel of John, which lacks what has become known as the institutional narrative for the Eucharist, contains the Bread of

5. See Carmignac, *Recherches*, 143–44.

Life Discourse that deepens the meaning of bread as a sign for Jesus himself:

I am the bread of life. Your fathers ate the manna in the wilderness, and they died. This is the bread which comes down from heaven, that a man may eat of it and not die. I am the living bread which came down from heaven; if any one eats of this bread, he will live for ever; and the bread which I shall give for the life of the world is my flesh. (Jn 6:48–51)

The implications of this association between bread and the flesh of Jesus became a source of scandal to many of Jesus' contemporaries, who "disputed among themselves." The allusions to their Scriptures and the sheer physicality of the image inspired, at best, confusion, at worst, disgust: "For my flesh is food indeed, and my blood is drink indeed. He who eats my flesh and drinks my blood abides in me, and I in him" (Jn 6:55–56). The idea of gnawing upon the bread that is Jesus' flesh would repel some, but it would also draw others into the mysteries of the Passion and the Eucharist.

The Meaning of Epiousios

Any translation betrays the meaning of the original, since every language holds nuances that cannot be captured in another tongue. Yet, this becomes especially problematic when a word's true meaning in the original language remains unknown. The Lord's Prayer contains a word, *epiousios*, that puzzled even a brilliant native speaker, Origen of Alexandria. Origen noted that the word "is not employed by any of the Greek writers, nor by philosophers, nor by individuals in common usage, but seems to have been formed by the evangelists; at least Matthew and Luke concur in employing the term in an identical manner."[6] Matthew's Gospel offers, "Give to us today our *epiousion* (?) bread," while Luke's Gospel contains, "Give to us daily our *epiousion* (?) bread." What are we to make of this mysterious adjective?[7]

6. *De or.* 27.7, PG 11, 510C, in Stewart-Sykes, *Lord's Prayer*, 179.
7. C. Day notes that references to *epiousios* outside the New Testament are

Ulrich Luz summarizes five possible meanings for the Greek word *epiousios*:

(1) From the Greek prefix *epi*, "on, upon, over" and *ousia*, "being, substance." Thus, the prayer speaks of "bread that unites with our substance" or "bread that surpasses our substance."

(2) From the Greek word *ousia*, which can mean "existence or livelihood." The expression therefore means "bread necessary for existence."

(3) From an abbreviated form of the expression *epi tēn ousan (hēmeran)*. We seek bread "for today."

(4) From the verb *epienai*, "to come to." We therefore ask for "bread for the coming day."

(5) Again, from the verb *epienai*, but this time in reference to "the coming age": "bread for the coming age; bread for the future."[8]

Cases for and against these meanings can be made, though most modern scholars tend to rule out the first.

What to do? Many of the Fathers were aware of the issues surrounding *epiousios* and each Father supported his preferred meaning or meanings. Origen, for instance, reviewed the known possibilities and generously allowed them *all* to share the stage. Thus, moving forward into the teachings of the ancients, we too should remain open to the potential of a term that leads us deeper into the various mysteries.

---

works discussing the Lord's Prayer. Papyri purported to contain the word are highly disputed; Day, "In Search of the Meaning of *Epiousios* in the Lord's Prayer: Rounding Up the Usual Suspects," *Acta Patristica et Byzantina* 14 (2003): 97. Also see Black, *Lord's Prayer*, 150–56.

8. Luz, *Matthew*, 319–20. Also see Day, "In Search of the Meaning of *Epiousios*," 97–111. In a recent article, Anthony Harvey argues that the word indicates "bread that is sufficient for the day"—that is, we must only pray for bread that we need and we should not be greedy for surplus; Harvey, "Daily Bread," *Theological Studies* 69 (April 2018): 25–38.

The Bread of the Fathers

The Fathers' treatment of "bread" in the Lord's Prayer can be divided into material and spiritual interpretations. In general, they had no problem with accepting *both* types of interpretations simultaneously, since God's Word always admits multiple meanings.

Material Interpretations

Since bread represents the basic needs of human existence—it is the bare minimum for sustaining life—the petition teaches one to limit desires to the essentials of life. Maximus the Confessor memorably summarizes this point: "Let us prove that we eat to live and let us not be convicted of living to eat. For one is clearly proper to a rational nature and the other to a nature without reason."[9] Thus, Christians distinguish themselves in the world by refusing to pursue superfluous things. Tertullian writes, "For he [Christ] commands us to ask for the bread which is all that the faithful require."[10] One must therefore embrace a daily form of asceticism: simplicity of life devoid of unnecessary material things.

The petition also inspires a personal abandonment to divine providence. Jesus himself taught, "Look at the birds of the air: they neither sow nor reap nor gather into barns, and yet your heavenly Father feeds them. Are you not of more value than they?" (Mt 6:26). The request for bread therefore becomes an act of trust in the loving Father. One is in fact praying, "O God, I trust that you will provide me with the basic needs of life." Cyprian reminds his audience through scriptural citations that "the just man will not go without daily food, as it is written: 'The Lord will not allow the just man to starve' (Prv 10:3), and again: 'I have been young and now I am old, and I have not seen the just man destitute nor his seed begging for bread' (Ps 36:25)."[11] Fur-

---

9. *Or. dom.*, CCG 23, 62, lines 612–13, in Berthold, *Maximus*, 114.

10. *De oratione* 6, PL 1, 1161A, in Stewart-Sykes, *Lord's Prayer*, 47.

11. *De oratione dom.* 21, PL 4, 533B–34A, in Stewart-Sykes, *Lord's Prayer*, 80.

thermore, since Christ has promised the coming of the kingdom, the disciple should not show excessive concern for the future, but rather he should rely upon God's providence day by day. "Very properly, therefore, does the disciple of Christ, who is forbidden to give consideration for the morrow, ask for sustenance for himself for that one day. It would be a contradictory and negative thing were we, who ask that the kingdom of God come quickly, to seek to live a long time in the present age."[12] God will provide us with what we need now; we should not become overly anxious about tomorrow.

Spiritual Interpretations

Some of the Fathers argue that bread is a spiritual symbol. While one does trust in God's loving care regarding basic material needs, one should always look toward the higher goods that aid man in reaching his authentic end. Thus, this "super-substantial" (*epiousion*) bread points beyond its material limitations toward deeper truths regarding the participation in the life of the Creator.

First, the bread may symbolize the gift of God's wisdom to the soul. God made man in his image, and this image manifests itself in the exercise of the intellect, which distinguishes man from all other living creatures. That which forms the mind and spirit, divine Wisdom, therefore aids the growth into the divine likeness. Origen writes, "And the bread is that which gives nourishment to the true humanity, which is made in the image of God, and so whoever is so nourished grows into the likeness of the Creator. What is more nourishing to the soul than reason? And what is more precious to the mind of whoever receives it than the wisdom of God? And what is more agreeable to the rational nature than truth?"[13]

Second, the bread may be the Word of God—that is, the

---

12. *De oratione dom.* 19, PL 4, 532B–33A, in Stewart-Sykes, *Lord's Prayer*, 79.
13. *De or.* 27.2, PL 11, 505D, in Stewart-Sykes, *Lord's Prayer*, 176.

Scriptures as they are proclaimed and preached in the life of the Church. Thus, Augustine taught, "our daily food on this earth is the Word of God, which is always being dispensed in the churches; our reward when the labor is done—that is called life everlasting."[14] It is in the life of the Church that the Christian receives the real nourishment for union with God the Father, since the Church has the mission of proclaiming the Gospel message. The bishops and priests therefore have the great responsibility of distributing the food for eternal life in their preaching, teaching, and living of the Scriptures, the Word of God.

Finally, the bread may be Christ himself. On the one hand, some Fathers make a direct identification with the person of Christ: the disciple receives a form of participation in the life of the risen Lord. Tertullian gives voice to this spiritual sharing in Christ's life:

Nonetheless, we should understand "Give us this day our daily bread" better in a spiritual sense. For Christ is our bread, because Christ is life and bread is life. "I am," he said, "the bread of life" (Jn 6:35). And a little earlier, "The bread is the word of the living God who came down from the heavens" (Jn 6:48). Then because his body is accounted bread, "This is my body" (Mt 26:6). Therefore, when we ask for our daily bread, we are asking that we should perpetually be in Christ and that we should not be separated from his body.[15]

This participation in the Lord is a privilege of the Christian. "For Christ is the bread of life (Jn 6:48), and thus he is not the bread of anyone but ourselves," wrote Cyprian.[16] Reception of the bread that is Christ, though a privilege of the Christian, demands a state of life worthy for participation.

On the other hand, the symbol of bread also alludes to Christ in the celebration of the Eucharist. In the Mass, the faithful en-

---

14. *Serm.* 56.10, PL 38, 381, in Kavanagh, *Commentary*, 248.
15. *De oratione* 6, PL 1, 1160A–61A, in Stewart-Sykes, *Lord's Prayer*, 46.
16. *De oratione dom.* 18, PL 4, 531A, in Stewart-Sykes, *Lord's Prayer*, 78.

counter the real presence of the Lord who surrendered himself upon the cross. Peter Chrysologus preaches a continuity between the incarnate Son and the One who offers himself to and for the Church in the sacred liturgy: "He himself is the bread who was placed in the virgin, fermented in the flesh, completed in the passion, baked in the oven of the tomb, and confected in the churches. Placed upon the altars, he gives the heavenly food daily to the faithful."[17]

Among the Western Fathers one finds a particular emphasis on the regular reception of the Eucharist. Augustine notes that the Eastern Church of his time did not encourage such a practice, but he then gives support for daily reception of the Eucharist in his own diocese.[18] Peter Chrysologus emphasizes the importance of the Eucharist for the future consummation in Christ: "But daily and on the day he wants us to ask for the viaticum of bread in the sacrament of his body, whereby from this we might come to the perpetual day and to the table itself of Christ, and, as we have taken a taste from here, there we may seize the fullness and all satisfaction."[19] Cyprian highlights the ethical import of the desire to receive the consecrated bread daily: one must avoid sin and seek purity to partake of the Eucharist.

Furthermore, we ask that this bread be given to us daily, lest we who are in Christ and receive the Eucharist daily as the food of salvation, when some more serious fault intervenes, should, while separated and not communicating, be prohibited from the heavenly bread and thus

17. *Col. serm.* 67.7, CCL 24A, 404–5, lines 58–61.
18. "Although this bread is called a daily bread, in the Eastern countries there are very many who do not partake of the Lord's Supper every day; nevertheless, they occasion no scandal by not partaking. They are not condemned as disobedient, for their ecclesiastical superiors do not command them partake. Therefore, in those regions, the sacramental Bread is not understood as daily bread; if it were so understood, then those who do not partake of it every day would be charged with the guilt of grave sin"; *De serm. Dom.* II.7.26, CCL 25, 114–15, lines 537–46, in Kavanagh, *Lord's Prayer*, 133. Also see *Serm.* 57.7, PL 38, 390.
19. *Col. serm.* 68.7, CCL 24A, 409, lines 84–88.

separated from the body of Christ.... "If you do not eat of the flesh of the Son of Man and drink his blood, you will not have life in you" (Jn 6:53). And therefore we ask that our bread, that is Christ, be given to us daily in order that we who remain and live in Christ might not fall away from his sanctification and body.[20]

In the end, all of the Fathers' spiritual interpretations flow from the person of Christ, the One who is Word, Wisdom, and the Bread of Life. The petition asks God the Father to give us a share in the life of the Son—a share that will find its fulfillment in the coming of the kingdom.

The Fathers and *Epiousios*

Both Origen and Jerome offer detailed linguistic analyses of *epiousios* that still remain valid and suggestive.[21] They provide various interpretations—"beyond substance," "coming," "future"— but in general they believe that the word indicates the superior and transformative nature of the mysterious bread. For these gifted commentators, the translation "supersubstantial" summarizes all the spiritual meanings examined in the previous section. Thus Origen declares, "The 'supersubstantial' bread, therefore, is that which corresponds most closely to the rational nature, and is related to its essence, bringing about health and well-being and strength in the soul and, since the word of God is im-

20. *De oratione dom.* 18, PL 4, 531A–B.
21. Jerome, for instance, speculated on the Hebrew origins and examined non-canonical variants. "'Give us this day our supersubstantial bread.... We have therefore carefully examined the Hebrew and wherever they had used *periousion* and we found *sogolla*, which Symmachus translated *exaireton*, that is, 'special' or 'surpassing,' although it is interpreted in one place as 'extraordinary.' When therefore we ask God to give us 'extraordinary' or 'special' bread, we ask him who said: 'I am the bread which descended from heaven.' In the gospel which is called *According to the Hebrews*, I found *maar* applied to 'supersubstantial bread,' which means 'tomorrow,' thereby having this sense: Our tomorrow—that is, future—bread give us today"; *In Matt.* I.6.11, SC 242, 130–132, lines 60–74.

mortal, communicating its own immortality to anyone who eats it."[22] Jerome defined the supersubstantial bread as "that which is beyond all substances and surpasses all creatures."[23] Though we must certainly pray for material necessities, Jesus also wants his disciples to hunger for food that transcends the limits of material existence.

This spiritual food changes the faithful to their very core. Cyril of Jerusalem taught the new members of his flock, "The common bread is not super-substantial bread, but this Holy Bread is super-substantial, that is, appointed for the substance of the soul. For this bread 'goes not into the belly and is cast out into the draught,' but is diffused through all you are, for the benefit of body and soul."[24] *Epiousios*, according to John Cassian, describes both the transformative nature of the bread and its necessity in the life of the Church:

Give us this day our *epiousion*—that is, supersubstantial—"bread," which another evangelist has referred to as "daily." The former indicates the noble quality of this substance, which places it above all other substances and which, in the sublimity of its magnificence and power to sanctify, surpasses every creature, whereas the latter expresses the nature of its use and its goodness. For when it says "daily," it shows that we are unable to attain the spiritual life on a day without it.[25]

Epiousios therefore describes the bread that is Christ himself—whether in the Eucharist or through the indwelling of Christ's Spirit. Christians require this nourishment for their daily existence in the Lord.

---

22. *De or.* 9, PL 11, 514A, in Stewart-Sykes, *Lord's Prayer*, 180–81.
23. *In Matt.* I.6.11, SC 242, 130–32, lines 60–74.
24. Cyril of Jeruslaem, *Catacheses* V.15, PG 33, 1120B, in Cross, *Lectures*, 76.
25. *Col.* IX.21.1, PL 49, 794A–95A, in Ramsey, *Conferences*, 343.

Conclusion: The Fathers and the Bread of Life

For the Fathers, the Word of God cannot be confined to one meaning. As a seed planted in the field of the Church, it bears a variety of fruits fitting for every age. This petition—"Give us this day our daily bread"—opens up mysteries at the heart of Christian life.

First, the petition for daily bread calls for a simplicity of life. All Christians, not just monks, should embrace basic ascetical practices—fasting, the avoidance of superfluous wealth, the limiting of sensual pleasures—for the sake of a full dedication to God. Bread comes to symbolize these disciplines, since it expresses the raw, essential need of the human person for sustenance: we eat to live, we do not live to eat. Thus, in this request we ask for the grace to live daily for God and not to become distracted by disordered desires.

Second, by regularly expressing this authentic desire for a basic need, we grow in dependence on divine providence. This does not mean that we abandon our worldly responsibilities in favor of letting God take care of everything, since this would be an attempt to make God our servant. Yet, we should not let the preoccupations and anxieties for our material sustenance distract us. God's providence works toward a greater goal—the salvation of souls, the deification of the human person. In this case, the symbol of bread reminds us that God will care for us in our true need—that is, the grace to complete our pilgrimage and enter the household of the Father. We should not worry about what we are to eat and what we are to wear because the Father will provide us with even greater things that will contribute to life in the kingdom.

Third, in seeking bread from the Father, we in fact seek Christ. "I am the bread of life." Christ nourishes the faithful as Word, as Wisdom, and as the Bread of Life broken in the Eucharist. While physical bread becomes part of the one who consumes it, the one who eats super-substantial bread becomes one with Christ. And we need this bread *daily* in its various forms. Thus, we seek a purity of heart that will allow for the beneficial reception of Christ that we might become more fully incorporated into his life.

Is the Bread of Life for today, or tomorrow, or the age to come? In fact, it is bread for all times and ages. We require this bread to sanctify the moment and become holy in the present circumstances. We need this nourishment to find the courage and clarity to confront the exigencies of the coming day. And we hunger for this bread because it forms us in the hope of the coming kingdom, when all desires will be fulfilled.

8

SEVENTH *APORIA*

CAN WE MAKE A DEAL WITH GOD?

The second "we petition" seems relatively straightforward: if we want to receive God's forgiveness, we must practice forgiveness in our own lives. God has pardoned us, so we must do the same with others. Jesus's story about the unmerciful servant makes it clear how this relationship works: A king forgives the debts of a servant, refusing to sell the man into slavery as payment. Yet, when that servant meets a fellow servant who is in debt to him, he has the man cast into prison. The king, hearing of this lack of charity, has the unmerciful servant brought before him and rebukes him severely and casts him into prison: "You wicked servant! I forgave you all that debt because you pleaded with me; and should not you have had mercy on your fellow servant, as I had mercy on you?" (Mt 18:32–33). We, therefore, who have received God's mercy, should imitate God's love when dealing with others.

Yet, a closer examination of this petition reveals difficulties. While the parable calls for the servant to imitate his master in forgiveness, the petition calls for *the master to imitate the servant*: "Forgive … as we forgive." In effect, we establish a quid pro quo or *do ut det* relationship with the Creator—that is, "something for something" or "I give that he might give." God forgives us *because* we forgave others. As Gregory of Nyssa writes, we apparently make a deal with God and tell God to follow our example: "May you do what I have done, Lord. Lord, imitate your servant!"[1]

Is this really what the petition is saying? Are we really asking the Creator of the universe to follow *our* standards and example? Is it right to say that we are making a deal with God? The solutions to this problem once again open up new possibilities for appropriating the Lord's Prayer.

A Puzzling Petition

The Two Versions of the Petition

A comparison between the two versions of the prayer reveals significant nuances. First, Matthew has, "And forgive us our debts, as we too forgave (have forgiven) our debtors." The verb "forgave" is a Greek aorist, implying a completed action that takes place *before* God forgives: "Father, forgive our debts as we have already done with others." Luke, however, uses a present tense for the second verb: "And forgive us our sins, for we ourselves also forgive each one who is in debt to us." Thus, Luke suggests a continuous action that is simultaneous with God's definitive (aorist tense) act of forgiveness: "Father, forgive us while we, at the same time, are regularly forgiving others."

Second, Matthew speaks of "debts" and "debtors," a possible reflection of the Aramaic (*hôbâ*), which can mean both debt and sin.[2] Luke, however, may have adapted the prayer for a gentile audience that was not familiar with the Jewish use of "debt" as a metaphor for a transgression against one's neighbor or God.

1. *De or. dom.* 5, GNO 7.2, 61, lines 14–24; 62, lines 14–16.
2. See Albright and Mann, *Matthew*, 76; Fitzmyer, *Luke*, 897; Gary Anderson, *Sin: A History* (New Haven, Conn.: Yale University Press, 2009), 31–33.

Thus, he begins with "forgive us our sins" (*harmatia*), followed by the participle of the verb "to owe" or "to be in debt": "Forgive each one in debt to us." This relationship that Luke clearly establishes between debts and sins will greatly shape the interpretations of the Fathers.

Finally, there is the puzzle regarding the relationship between "forgive our debts"/"forgive us our sins" and "as we too forgave"/"for we also forgive." Matthew creates a very strict relationship between the two through the Greek *hōs kai*, "as we *too* forgive," while Luke seems to mitigate the connection through the Greek *kai gar*, "for also" or "because also." The Matthean variant particularly presents, in the words of Jean Carmignac, a "singular theological boldness," since it implies that man's act of forgiveness must take place before that of God's and therefore *brings about* God's response.[3] Even the Lukan variant suggests a causal relationship in which God's mercy is a direct result of man's.[4]

Together, then, these two versions present interesting, if not disturbing, problems to the Fathers: the equating of sin and debt and the relationship between human and divine forgiveness.

Winning God's Forgiveness?

Contemporary scholars generally respond to the strange relationship between human and divine forgiveness in four different ways: the exchange model, the precondition model, the eschatological model, and the exemplar model. In the exchange model, we forgive our debtors in order to obtain God's pardon. This is the *do ut det*—I give in order that he might give—solution. Thus, God can be "bought" through an anterior act of forgive-

---

3. Carmignac, *Recherches*, 231.
4. I. H. Marshall insists that Luke avoids the quid pro quo suggested in Matthew via his use of the particle *gar*, though the causal relationship still remains; see Marshall, *The Gospel of Luke* (Grand Rapids, Mich.: Eerdmans, 1978), 461.

ness. Though most scholars reject this approach,[5] Gary Anderson does suggest a mitigated version. When we say "as we forgive our debtors," we in effect make a promise that occurs simultaneously with the petition for God's forgiveness: "Forgiveness here is imagined as a gracious act of refusing to collect on an obligation. The person praying asks that God act this way, while at the same time affirming an intention to do the same."[6] Essentially the petitioner declares, "Forgive me Lord, and I shall do the same," making the anteriority of man's forgiveness, which is implied by the aorist in Matthew's version, an anticipated payment for the divine pardon.

Most scholars understand the relationship to be a precondition. The petitioner must acquire a certain personal disposition—that of the merciful servant—before he can ask for divine forgiveness or before he can even be open to receiving pardon. The forgiveness of sins creates a necessary "manner of being" in the person who desires to approach God and to receive God's pardon. R. Alan Culpepper writes, "One who will not forgive cannot receive forgiveness, mercy flows through the same channel, whether being given or received. There is no *quid pro quo* here; however, the ability to forgive and be forgiven is part of the same gift."[7]

The eschatological model is a variation of the preceding response. As noted in chapter one, the Lord's Prayer may be interpreted as an anticipation of and preparation for the end times—that is, the fullness of divine adoption will only be achieved in the

5. For instance, see Fitzmyer, *Luke*, 899; Heinz Schürmann, *Das Gebet des Herrn als Schlüssel zum Verstehen Jesu* (Leipzig: Herder, 1990), 123–24.

6. Anderson, *Sin*, 31.

7. R. Alan Culpepper, *Luke* (Nashville, Tenn.: Abingdon, 1995), 235. Joachim Jeremias also writes, "Thus the second half of the second petition is a self-reminder of one's own forgiveness, a declaration of readiness to pass on God's forgiveness. As Jesus continually stresses, this readiness is the indispensable prior condition for God's forgiveness"; Jeremias, *New Testament Theology*, trans J. Bowden (London: Redwood, 1972), 1:201. Also see Lohmeyer, *Lord's Prayer*, 186; Fitzmyer, *Luke*, 899.

consummation of all things in Christ. Thus, one's forgiveness of debts anticipates and reflects the divine remission of debts or sins that will take place at the end of history. This disposition, forged through the daily forgiveness of others, represents the state one desires to be in at the time of judgment.[8] One's mercy toward others represents a form of "realized eschatology"—signs of the end times taking place even now—in the anticipation of the full remission of sins in the Second Coming.

The last solution, the exemplar model, remains the most controversial: man presents himself to God as an example or model by essentially saying, "O God, do as I am doing." R. H. Gundry boldly defends this position when he states that the petition is "a paradigm of forgiveness rather than a reason for forgiveness, i.e. forgiveness of others presents God with an example of the forgiveness sought from him, not with a meritorious act by which God's forgiveness might be earned."[9] Yet, an important question remains: How can creatures become models for the Creator?

The Meaning of Debts

The Old Testament and early rabbinic literature often portrayed transgressions against God and neighbor as "a bond of indebtedness deducted from one's balance sheet."[10] When the people turned from God, they failed to give God the obedience and worship that was due. This debt accrued to God often required a form of repayment through trial and suffering, though God's love remained ever ready to pardon what was owed. Thus, Isaiah proclaims hope to the people:

---

8. For examples of this approach, see Raymond Brown, "*Pater Noster*," 203; M. Eugene Boring, *The Gospel of Matthew* (Nashville, Tenn.: Abingdon, 1995), 204–5; Davies and Allison, *Matthew*, 612; Schürmann, *Das Gebet*, 124.

9. Gundry, *Matthew*, 108–9.

10. Anderson, *Sin*, 20.

Comfort, comfort my people, says your God.
Speak tenderly to Jerusalem,
and cry to her
that their warfare is ended,
that her iniquity is pardoned,
that she has received from the Lord's hand
double for all her sins. (Is 40:1–2)

In addition to asking God for pardon of individual sins, this petition in the Lord's Prayer is also "situating forgiveness within the broader covenantal context of the eschatological jubilee and the new exodus."[11] The jubilee year was a time given for both the forgiveness of debts and return to one's land or property: "And you shall hallow the fiftieth year, and proclaim liberty throughout the land to all its inhabitants; it shall be jubilee for you, when each of you shall return to his property and each of you shall return to his family" (Lv 25:10–11).[12] Yet, it also became symbolic of a future restoration of Israel and a forgiveness of its debts to God: a new Exodus was coming in which captives would be set free. Thus, Isaiah speaks of the year of the Lord's favor, a jubilee:

The Spirit of the Lord God is upon me,
because the Lord has anointed me
to bring good tidings to the afflicted;
He has sent me to bind up the brokenhearted
to proclaim liberty to the captives,
and the opening of the prison to those who are bound;
to proclaim the year of Lord's favor.... (Is 61:1–2)

In turn, this hope for liberation from debt and a return to the land would become associated with the eschatological hope for the coming of the Messiah—the one who would bring about

---

11. Brant Pitre, *Jesus and the Last Supper* (Grand Rapids, Mich.: Eerdmans, 2015), 182.

12. Pitre, *Last Supper*, 179.

the great year of jubilee.[13] This petition, therefore, may echo the hope of the people not only for freedom from sin, but also for a coming fulfillment, the kingdom of God. Their forgiveness of debts—both sins and monetary debts—inaugurated a new life and order in union with God.

Forgiveness and the Fathers

Creation in Debt

The Fathers interpret the significance of "debts" in the Lord's Prayer in several ways. First, some assume a literal interpretation: a debt indicates a monetary sum that one owes to a creditor. Augustine takes a radical stance toward such debt forgiveness, calling for Christians to offer a full pardon even in the cases of deadbeats and the irresponsible:

> A monetary debt, therefore, is to be remitted to one who is unwilling to pay of his own accord or refuses to pay it on demand, for his refusal may be due to the fact that he has not wherewith to pay, or to the fact that he is avaricious and covetous. Each of these reasons arises from a lack of something: the former, from a lack of means; the latter, from a lack of character. Therefore, whoever remits a debt to such a man remits it to one in need. He performs a Christian act, for he observes the rule that he ought to be willing to lose what is due to him.[14]

The Christian should be free of material desires and therefore indifferent to what is owed to him. Since even the just pursuit of payment leads to a form of covetousness in the heart, the creditor should erase monetary debts from the ledger.

Second, "debt" suggests the contingency of human existence. No one is the source of his own being, and no one sustains himself in existence. Instead, there is a network of "debts" that unites

13. On evidence from the Dead Sea Scrolls, see Pitre, *Last Supper*, 180–81.

14. *De serm. Dom.*, CCL 35, 117, lines 601–8, in Kavanagh, *Commentary*, 136.

all contingent beings. Origen, for instance, offers a profound reflection on this often-overlooked truth. We are indebted to fellow citizens and the human race in general for daily support in all stages of life.[15] We depend upon God for the gifts of our bodies and souls.[16] We owe due homage and love to the Trinity for the divine *philanthropia*, or love of humanity: "And we are also debtors to Christ, who bought us with his own blood, just as every house-servant is a debtor to the one who purchased him on account of the great sum that was paid for him. And there is a certain debt we that we pay back to the Holy Spirit, whenever we do not grieve the Holy Spirit, in whom we have been sealed for the day of redemption (Eph 4:30)."[17] We should also be conscious of what we owe our guardian angel who protects us in life: "Even if we do not know clearly who the angel of each one of us is—the one who looks upon the face of the Father in heaven (Mt 18:10)—nonetheless it is apparent to each one of us examining the matter that we are also debtors in some ways to each angel."[18] Thus, there is never a moment in which we are not in debt to others, and, vice versa, there are constantly persons who are in debt to us for our contributions to society.

A full awareness of this truth—our continual status as debtors—enlightens us to the fact that all are debtors and no one is strictly a creditor. "Indeed, it is impossible for one in this life not to be in debt every hour of the night and day."[19] Humbled by our very mode of existence, we should express mercy and forgiveness toward our fellow debtors at all stages of life.

Finally, the Fathers, in keeping with the version of Luke, interpret "debt" as sin. This petition therefore teaches a fundamental truth: all are sinners. Even when these sins are not great acts of

---

15. *De or.* 28.2, PG 11, 522B–C.
16. *De or.* 28.2, PG 11, 522B–C.
17. *De or.* 28.3, PG 11, 524B.
18. *De or.* 28.3, PG 11, 524B.
19. *De or.* 28.4, PG 11, 525A. Also see Augustine, *Serm.* 58.5, PL 38, 395.

evil, such as murder or adultery, the accumulated peccadillos become a weight that draws one away from God. "Lead is one compact mass; sand is composed of many grains, but it crushes you by their multitude. Your sins are small; yet, do you not see that from tiny drops rivers are filled and lands are lessened? Our sins are small, but they are many."[20] Every time one makes this petition, he should recall his sinful state and need for divine pardon:

How necessarily, how properly and prudently, are we reminded that we are sinners and are under obligation to ask on account of our sins so that, whilst the mercy of God is being sought, the mind may be recalled to a sense of its guilt. Lest anyone be self-satisfied, thinking himself innocent, and should perish once again because of his boasting, he is informed and instructed daily that he is a sinner, being commanded to make prayer daily on account of his sins.[21]

Yet this petition also reminds us that the pardon of sins is possible even after passing through the saving waters of baptism. For some Fathers, the question of post-baptismal reconciliation in the early Church found its response in this petition. Thus, John Chrysostom writes that "it is perfectly clear that He introduced this rule of supplication, as knowing, and signifying, that it is possible even after the Font to wash ourselves from our offences."[22] In fact, the baptized must *regularly* seek forgiveness for their sins to avoid falling into total corruption: "But, as to those who are baptized and then continue to live—these contract some imperfection through the frailty of mortals. Even though the ship is not lost through these imperfections, the pumps must be used, for if the pumps are not used, there is a gradual leakage that may sink the whole ship. By making this petition, we make use of the pumps."[23] Jesus therefore teaches that God desires the salvation

20. *Serm.* 56.12, PL 38, 383, in Kavanagh, *Commentary*, 251.
21. *De oratione dom.* 22, PL 4, 534C–35A, in Stewart-Sykes, *Lord's Prayer*, 81.
22. *In Matthaeum* 19, 280–81, in Prevost, *Matthew*, 297.
23. *Serm.* 56.11, PL 38, 382, in Kavanagh, *Commentary*, 249.

of every sinner: "A confession is a request for pardon, because whoever asks pardon confesses a wrongdoing. So it is shown that penitence is acceptable to God because he desires this, rather than the death of a sinner."[24]

How Can We Ask God to Imitate Us?

How do the Fathers deal with the curious form of the petition? First, some Fathers believe that the petition calls for the formation of a receptive and obedient disposition toward God. "Forgive ... as we forgive" actually indicates that our disposition toward forgiveness will become the criterion for our future judgment. Augustine makes it clear to his catechumens that this formation must begin from the moment they enter the font: "You are about to be baptized; forgive everything. Whatever anyone of you has in his heart against anyone let him dismiss it from his heart. Come to the font with this disposition, then rest assured that you are forgiven all the sins that you have contracted—both the sin that is yours by reason of birth from parents with original sin according to Adam ... and also whatever sins you may have committed during your lives."[25] Cyprian teaches that this attitude must remain throughout one's life: "The Lord instructs you, therefore, to be peaceable and agreeable and of one mind in his house. He wishes that we should remain as we are when we are reborn in our second birth, that those who are children of God should remain in the peace of God, and that those who are in possession of one spirit should possess one mind and heart."[26] The merciful disposition of a person then becomes the measure of one's fidelity toward God in the final judgment. According to John Chrysostom, we become our own judges—God will forgive us as we forgave others: "So that the beginning is of us, and

24. *De oratione* 7, PL 1, 1162A, in Stewart-Sykes, *Lord's Prayer*, 47.
25. *Serm.* 56, 13, PL 38, 385, in Kavanagh, *Commentary*, 251.
26. *De oratione dom.* 23, PL 4, 535C, in Stewart-Sykes, *Lord's Prayer*, 82–83.

we ourselves have control over the judgment that is to be passed upon us. For in order that no one, even of the senseless, might have any complaint to make, either great or small, when brought to judgment; on you, who are to give account, He causes the sentence to depend."[27]

Yet, some Fathers do accept the idea of making a pact or covenant with God. God condescends ("descends to be with us"), just as he did with the Israelites, in order to form a covenant with the baptized. Peter Chrysologus preaches, "He asks that so much be given to him, to be forgiven to the extent that he himself forgives. And he gives pleasure to the Lord, and he [the one praying the petition] thus invites God into an agreement (*pactus*)."[28] And Cyril of Jerusalem declares, "And we enter into a covenant with God, entreating Him to pardon our sins, as we also forgive our neighbors their debts."[29] Every time one makes this petition, one renews a pact with God and binds himself to the way of mercy. John Chrysostom notes that many are aware of the awesome nature of this agreement between creature and Creator: "Some people fear this, and when this prayer is recited together in church by the whole congregation they pass over this line in silence, lest by their own words they obligate rather than excuse themselves."[30] Like the covenants of old, the failing in one's obligations toward God will lead to terrible consequences. Yet, the petition also contains the hope of reconciliation with God and neighbor.

Perhaps the most radical answer to this *aporia* comes from Gregory of Nyssa, who concludes that we do indeed become models for God: God imitates our acts of forgiveness. How does Gregory justify such a response?

First, Gregory argues that one who wishes to ask God pardon for debts must become *like God*. One grows in the divine like-

---

27. *In Matthaeum* XIX.281, in Prevost, *Commentary*, 297.
28. *Col. serm.* 68.8, CCL 24A, 410, lines 90–93.
29. *Catacheses* 16, PG 33, 1120C, in Cross, *Lectures*, 35–36, 76–77.
30. *Col.* IX.22.4, PL 49, 797B–98A, in Ramsey, *Conferences*, 344.

ness by acquiring the virtues, which reflect the qualities of God. Therefore, when one shows mercy, one manifests the divine quality, or virtue, of mercy and becomes more like God:

For [Jesus] delineates through the words of the prayer what sort of man he desires to approach God: Such a man is no longer manifested by the definitions of human nature, but is similar to God himself through virtue, so that he seems to be another god by doing the things which God alone can do. For the forgiveness of debts belongs to God alone, since it is exclusive to Him: "No one is able to forgive sins except God alone" (Mk 2:7). If indeed anyone should imitate in his own life the characteristics of divine nature, he becomes that which he has shown visibly by imitation. What does the prayer teach? First to take up bold speech through deeds and then to request amnesty from wrongs committed.[31]

Gregory then moves on to the most radical part of his solution: when we acquire the likeness of God, we now may become exemplars for the Creator. Since one must become similar to God in order to approach him, he can now act as a paradigm for God's mercy. By visibly demonstrating divine qualities—the virtues—one may ask God to be more generous than he, the human, was toward others.

For what is being said? Just as God is placed before those looking toward the good as an object of imitation—as St. Paul said, *be my imitators as I am Christ's* (1 Cor 11:1)—so again he desires that your disposition be an exemplar for God in respect to the good. In this way the order has been overturned so as to dare and, just as the good is fulfilled in us by imitation of God, so also to hope that God may imitate our actions whenever we do something good, as if you were to say to God: "May you do what I have done! Lord, imitate your servant.... I have shown a little love for man, since my nature does not contain much. But you show as much as you wish, since your power does not inhibit your generosity."[32]

31. *De or. dom.* 5, GNO 7.2, 59, lines 2–13.
32. *De or. dom.* 5, GNO 7.2, 72, line 8.

In effect, God "imitates" himself as he is reflected in the divine likeness found in man. Moreover, God will "outdo" man with a reciprocal response of generosity. By living according to the divine likeness, man's entire life becomes an advocate for his words and a petition for God's mercy.[33]

Maximus the Confessor also advances this model of imitation. The growth in divine likeness through an imitation of God can work the other way around—one who is like God can become an exemplar for God: "And man establishes himself as an exemplar for God, if one can say it, commanding the inimitable one to come and imitate him, saying, 'Forgive us our debts, as we forgive our debtors.'"[34] Thus, the boldness of the petition comes from one's growth in holiness and the divine likeness.

Conclusion: Forgive Us Our Sins and Debts

The petition for forgiveness in the Lord's Prayer is grounded in the relationship between humanity and the Creator. First, forgiveness is possible because the human person has been made in the image and likeness of God. Though sin has stained the beauty of this image, the grace of baptism restores it to its glory. Man continues to struggle with sin in his life, but God still offers the pardon that both maintains the image and enables man to grow in the divine likeness. God's forgiveness therefore redounds to God's glory by rendering the human person a luminous icon of the divine.

Second, forgiveness becomes possible in an act of divine "condescension," God's *descent to be with* humanity. In a mysterious way, God humbles himself and enters into a covenant with fallen humanity: "Forgive one another and I will do the same."

33. *De or. dom.* 5, GNO 7.2, 72, lines 8–9.
34. *Or. dom.* 4, CCG 23, 64, lines 651–53. For a fuller treatment of this theme, see John Gavin, SJ, "Becoming an Exemplar for God: Three Early Interpretations of Forgiveness in the Lord's Prayer," *Logos* 16, no. 3 (2013): 126–46.

Though God is the source of all forgiveness and healing, he nonetheless agrees to imitate what he sees reflected in the human image. The perfect form of condescension, the incarnation, effects and demonstrates this relationship: the pardon rendered visible by the Son on the Cross—"Forgive them, Father, for they know not what they do" (Lk 23:34)—becomes an exemplar for the Father, who in turn forgives fallen humanity. Now all persons may enter into Christ's pardon for his persecutors and become models for God.

Third, the forgiveness of others emerges from the unity of all in the body of Christ. Humans, as contingent beings, remain united in a network of debts and credits. But they now share an even deeper communion in the salvation that Christ won on the cross: all are one in the debt owed to Christ. The pardoning of debts erases the divisions that can mar this body and unites them in the love for God, while the common indebtedness to Christ becomes the liberation of all for divine union. Thus, this petition demands an examination of conscience in the context of the body of Christ. The Master writes, "Therefore before we hear these words of the Lord, brethren, let us first examine our hearts as to whether we are with justice asking of the Lord what we have not denied to those asking us."[35]

Finally, like all the petitions of the Lord's Prayer, the request for forgiveness points to the coming fulfillment of the kingdom. Our remission of debts and our reception of divine mercy in this time point toward the great jubilee year, the coming of Christ. We hope that, on the day of judgment, our debts will be remitted, and God's mercy will shine upon us.

35. *Regula*, SC 105, 312, lines 177–80, in Eberle, *Rule*, 99.

9

EIGHTH *APORIA*

The final petitions are traditionally rendered, "Lead us not into temptation (Greek: *peirasmos*), but deliver us from evil." This translation should certainly trouble us. Does God deliberately *tempt* us? Isn't temptation the devil's role? Surely the Creator does not desire to trick us into damnation!

The Fathers noted this problem in both the original Greek and in the Latin translations. Tertullian rejected outright the idea that God tries to lead us into evil: "Far be it that the Lord should seem to tempt, as though he were either ignorant of the faith of each of us, or sought to dethrone it, for weakness and malice are of the devil."[1] Origen, for his part, considered it strange that we would pray for deliverance from temptation at all, since trials are an essential part of this fallen existence: "Assuming that the Savior is not charging us to pray for the impossible, it seems to me to be worthwhile to explore how it is that we are ordered to request that we enter not into testing when the whole of human life is a time of testing."[2]

---

1. *De oratione* 8, PL 1, 1164A, in Stewart-Sykes, *Lord's Prayer*, 48.
2. *De or.* 29.1, PG 11, 530C–31A, in Stewart-Sykes, *Lord's Prayer*, 193.

More recently, Pope Francis, in a 2017 interview, suggested that "lead us not into temptation" should be changed to "do not let us fall into temptation"—a version already adopted in French and Spanish translations for its more nuanced theological and pastoral implications.[3] The pope's words, however, ignited an intense discussion among translators of the Bible, theologians, pastors, and laity.[4] Though views regarding the possible change vary greatly, the pope has rightly called attention to these problems of translation, theological significance, and pastoral care. The ancient questions of the Fathers have resurfaced in Pope Francis's voiced concern.

This petition therefore once again takes us into the mystery of theodicy: If God is just, why do evil, trials, and temptation exist in the world? If God does indeed tempt us into evil, while also delivering us from it, he seems to be both demonic and divine.

Trial or Temptation?

"Peirasmos" as Trial

One approach to resolving this *aporia* involves the meaning of the Greek word *peirasmos*: does *peirasmos* mean "trial," as in a period of testing, or "temptation," an attraction toward evil? A strong case can be made for "trial" or "test," a translation that would mitigate the interpretive problems considerably. The book of Sirach, for example, gives this advice regarding a friend: "When you gain a friend, gain him *through testing*, and do not trust him hastily" (Sir 6:7). A trial therefore reveals a person's virtues, such as fidelity, courage, and honor. A passage through hardships also

---

3. For the interview with Pope Francis, see https://www.youtube.com/watch?v=U16oJb33pfM.

4. For an overview of the recent controversy and suggested solutions, see Joshua Brotherton, "The 'Our Father' Translation Controversy," *Fellowship of Catholic Scholars Quarterly* 41, no. 3 (Fall 2018): 282–86.

strengthens one's character and exposes the weaknesses that must be overcome.

Numerous examples of trials occur in both the Old and the New Testaments. For example, the Israelites often *put God to the test* during their years of wandering in the desert. In their complaints the people, in effect, sought proof of God's fidelity toward them and his readiness to come to their aid. Such testing was, of course, presumptuous on the part of the Hebrew people; yet God generally did not abandon them in their stubbornness:

All the congregation of the sons of Israel moved on from the wilderness of Sin by stages, according to the commandment of the Lord, and camped at Reph'idim; but there was not water for the people to drink. Therefore, the people found fault with Moses, and said, "Give us water to drink." And Moses said to them, "Why do you find fault with me? *Why do you put the Lord to the test?*" (Ex 17:1-3)[5]

Second, God subjects the Patriarchs and the Hebrew people to trials in order to strengthen their fidelity and to aid them in overcoming weaknesses. God puts Abraham through a terrifying trial when he asks him to sacrifice his son, Isaac: "After these things *God tested* Abraham and said to him, 'Abraham!' And he said, 'Here am I.' He said, 'Take your son, your only-begotten son Isaac, whom you love, and go to the land of Mori'ah and offer him there as a burnt offering upon one of the mountains of which I shall tell you'" (Gn 22:1-2). In the book of Deuteronomy God explains the purpose of the people's years of wandering in the desert: "And you shall remember all the ways which the Lord your God has led you these forty years in the wilderness, *that he might humble you, testing you to know what was in your heart*, whether you would keep his commandments" (Dt 8:2). The Psalms regularly acknowledge that God tests those he loves:

5. On humanity's testing of God, see Kenneth Grayston, "The Decline of Temptation and the Lord's Prayer," *Scottish Journal of Theology* 46, no. 3 (August 1993): 294.

"*The Lord tests the righteous* and the wicked, and his soul hates him that loves violence" (Ps 11:5); "*For you, O God, have tested us; you have tried us as silver is tried*" (Ps 66:10).

This understanding of God's refining trials also appears in the New Testament. When Jesus explains the parable of the sower, he teaches that the wheat that landed on rocky ground are those that could not maintain fidelity during a period of trial: "And the ones on rock are those who, when they hear the word, receive it with joy; but these have not root, they believe for a while and in time of *trial* (*peirasmou*) fall away" (Lk 8:13). In another example, Jesus begs the disciples to stay awake during the eve of his Passion and pray for the strength to remain faithful during the period of strife:

And going a little farther he fell on his face and prayed, "My Father, if it be possible, let this chalice pass from me; nevertheless, not as I will, but as you will." And he came to the disciples and found them sleeping; and he said to Peter, "So could you not watch with me one hour? Watch and pray that you may not enter into *the test* (*peirasmon*); the spirit indeed is willing, but the flesh is weak." (Mt 26:40–41)

The incarnate Son took on our trials in life that he might save us from these very trials: "For because he himself has suffered and been tried, he is able to help those who are tried" (Heb 2:18).

Thus, the petition may refer to this tradition of divine trials that purify, refine, and strengthen the fidelity of God's beloved. This means that God uses suffering—suffering that emerged from man's fall into sin—to a positive end. In fact, growth through suffering allows both for man's free will and for the consequences of his choices. Even Christ embraced the way of trials in his mission from the Father and transformed them into redemptive experiences in union with his own passion.[6]

6. For an overview of the theme of "testing and trial," see Matteo Munari, "Fa'che non cadiamo," in *Studium Biblicum Franciscanum: Liber Annus LXIV*, ed. L. Daniel Chrupcala (Turnhout: Brepols, 2015), 166ff.

"*Peirasmos*" as Temptation

Peirasmos can also mean "temptation"—that is, a disordered attraction toward evil. Most often these temptations come in the form of trials that may drive one to abandon God or blaspheme. In fact, some of the divinely given trials reviewed above fall into this category: Abraham's mission to sacrifice his son; Jesus' temptation to reject the Father's will before his passion. Yet, most often the blandishments of the world serve as sufficient temptations for the faithful. "But those who desire to be rich fall into temptation (*peirasmon*), into a snare, into many senseless and hurtful desires that plunge men into the ruin and destruction. For the love of money is the root of all evils; it is through this raving that some have wandered away from the faith and pierced their hearts with many pangs" (1 Tm 6:9–10).

The devil also appears as one whom God *allows* to subvert justice in creation and lead humanity toward sin. The serpent that deceived Adam and Eve came to be recognized as the great tempter in later Jewish tradition. The book of Wisdom summarizes this interpretation:

> Thus they reasoned, but they were led astray,
> for their wickedness blinded them,
> and they did not know the secret purposes of God,
> nor hope for the wages of holiness,
> nor discern the prize for blameless souls;
> For God created man for incorruption,
> and made him in the image of his own eternity,
> but through the devil's envy death entered the world,
> and those who belong to his party experience it. (Ws 2:21–24)

In the book of Job, God allows Satan to impose a series of harsh trials upon the righteous Job in order to test his fidelity. The Satan of this book is not yet the demonic figure he will become in later tradition, but rather represents an "adversary" or "accuser" in the very court of God. Yet, he does function as a ruthless and merciless dealer of torture whom God permits to reign for a period in Job's life. The scene in which God places Job into Satan's hands disturbs the heart of any believer:

Then Satan answered the Lord, "Does Job fear God for nothing? Have you not put a hedge about him and his house and all that he has, on every side? You have blessed the work of his hands and his possessions have increased in the land. But put forth your hand now, and touch all that he has, and he will curse you to your face." And the Lord said to Satan, "Behold, all that he has is in your power; only upon himself do not put forth your hand." (Jb 1:9–12)

In the New Testament, the temptation of Jesus in the desert has inspired much commentary, including the chilling reflections that come from the mouth of the Grand Inquisitor in Dostoevsky's *The Brothers Karamazov*. The three synoptic Gospels present this scene (Mt 4:1–11; Mk 12:13; Lk 4:1–13), though only Mathew and Luke go into detail regarding the nature of the temptations. The devil's enticements—which differ in the order in Matthew and Luke—have puzzled commentators and scholars. Do they represent the various temptations of the Hebrew people in the desert: the complaints of hunger, the lack of fidelity and the desire for earthly security? Or perhaps they are rooted in anthropology: bread as a temptation for the body; power and false worship as disordered attractions for the spirit.

Whatever the interpretation, Luke makes it clear that the *Holy Spirit* leads Jesus into the desert: "And Jesus, full of the Holy Spirit, returned from the Jordan, and was led by the Spirit for forty days in the wilderness, tempted by the devil" (Lk 4:1–2). Thus, the Father seems to desire that Jesus face the adversary in spiritual combat. Furthermore, the devil even makes use of the Scriptures in his futile attempts to seduce the Son of God into revealing himself or into committing an act of rebellion.[7] The

7. Jesus, of course, responds in kind. On the apotropaic use of the Scriptures against evil forces, see Michael Morris, "Deuteronomy in the Matthean and Lukan

narrative ominously concludes with the promise of future battles: "And when the devil had ended every temptation (*peirasmon*), he departed from him until an opportune time" (Lk 4:13). This Gospel scene, more than any other, suggests that God may deliberately bring about temptations toward evil.

Yet, the Letter of James offers another understanding: God *allows* such blandishments and adversaries for the same reasons that he allows trials—that is, in order to strengthen free resolve and to purify from sin.[8]

Blessed is the man who endures temptation (*peirasmon*), for when he has stood the test he will receive the crown of life which God has promised to those who love him. Let no one say when he is tempted, "I am tempted by God"; for God cannot be tempted with evil and he himself tempts no one; but each person is tempted when he is lured and enticed by his own desire. Then desire when it has conceived gives birth to sin; and sin when it is full-grown brings forth death. (Jas 1:12–15)

Temptations and trials therefore come from man's own choices and disordered attractions. Yet, God allows the consequences of these sinful choices to act as teachers in the earthly pilgrimage.

The Evil One in the End Times

Some scholars try to resolve the problem of the final petition by putting it into an eschatological context: the temptation and the Evil One refer to the struggles of the end times. There are good reasons to embrace such an interpretation. First, while the Greek *apo tou ponērou* could be neuter—"from evil"—it is more likely a masculine form—"from the Evil One." Such use of the word can be found elsewhere in the Gospels. In the Gospel of Matthew,

---

Temptation in the Light of Early Jewish Antidemonic Tradition," *Catholic Biblical Quarterly* 78 (2016): 290–301.

8. On the interpretation of causative verbs expressing allowance, see Munari, "Fa'che non cadiamo," 172ff.

Jesus says, "When any one hears the word of the kingdom and does not understand it, *the Evil One* comes and snatches away what is sown in his heart; this is what was sown along the path" (Mt 13:19; also see Mt 13:38). Thus, the petition refers to the great and active adversary, the devil, and the desire to be liberated from his power.

Second, some New Testament verses speak of the coming final confrontation between God and the Evil One. In the Gospel of John, Jesus asks that the Father save his disciples from the devil: "I do not pray that you should take them out of the world, but that you should keep them from the *Evil One*" (Jn 17:15). In Revelation 3:10, Christ looks toward the coming showdown—a confrontation that can only end in the Evil One's total defeat: "Because you have kept my word of patient endurance, I will keep you from the hour of trial/temptation (*peirasmos*) which is coming on the whole world, to try those who dwell upon the earth." Paul encourages the Thessalonians to remain faithful in their anticipation of Christ's return: "But the Lord is faithful; he will strengthen you and guard you from the *Evil One*" (2 Thes 3:3).[9]

These petitions therefore ask for aid in preparing for the coming of Christ and the end of history. Christians place their trust in the Father to give them what they need when they will stand in judgment before Christ.

The Fathers on Trials and Temptations

The Nature of Temptation and Trials

In general, the Fathers do not make strict distinctions between *peirasmos* as "trial" or "temptation," seeing the term as a designation for the pervasive and destructive presence of evil in the world. *Peirasmos*, whether a trial or temptation, can lead one to a perversion of nature and the abandonment of God.

9. On this theme, see Raymond Brown, "*Pater Noster*," 204–8.

On the one hand, temptations come from the circumstances of the fallen world. Both disordered attractions and the enticements of corrupt men can lead one into personal trials. Theodore of Mopsuestia warns, "There are other things which assail us on unexpected occasions and involuntarily and strongly divert our choice and our mind from good things to ungodly things. This is especially the case with the opinions of unholy and contumelious men who are eager to do evil, because those (opinions) are very apt to divert us in one way or another from a thing with which we were pleased."[10]

On the other hand, the Fathers have a keen awareness of the Evil One's activity in the world. Maximus the Confessor had no illusions about the dangerous adversary in our midst. Man, by his own choice, entered into sin, but the devil continues to take advantage of man's wounded nature. Maximus the Confessor writes, "He here calls 'temptation' the law of sin which the first man did not bear when he came into existence, and 'evil' the devil, who mingled this law of sin with human nature and who by trickery persuaded man to transfer his soul's desire from what was permitted to what was forbidden, and to be turned around to transgress the divine commandment."[11] John Chrysostom also highlights both man's freedom and the seductions of the devil as the ongoing source of suffering in the world:

And He here calls the devil "the wicked one," commanding us to wage against him a war that knows no truce, and implying that he is not such by nature. For wickedness is not of those things that are from nature, but of them that are added by our own choice. And he is so called preeminently, by reason of the excess of his wickedness, and because he, in no respect injured by us, wages against us implacable war. Wherefore neither said He, "Deliver us from the wicked ones," but, "from the wicked one"; instructing us in no case to entertain displeasure against

10. Theodore of Mopsuestia, *Commentary on the Lord's Prayer*, trans. Mingana, 15.
11. *Or. dom.*, CCG 23, 67–68, lines 712–20, in Berthold, *Maximus*, 117.

our neighbors, for what wrongs so ever we may suffer at their hands, but to transfer our enmity from these to him, as being himself the cause of all our wrongs.[12]

Evil and temptation are therefore primarily associated with a malevolent intelligence, the devil, and the petition requests divine aid in this spiritual life-or-death conflict.

The Desert Fathers and Mothers—the Christians who embraced the radical life of asceticism in the desert during the early centuries of the Church—offered hard-won wisdom from their struggles with the Evil One and temptation. One Father in particular, Evagrius Ponticus, gave the tradition a remarkable series of insights on these themes.

Evagrius defines "temptation" as "the thought (*logismos*) of a monk that rises up through the passionate part of the soul and darkens the mind."[13] A temptation, therefore, is a "thought" that can emerge either from the disorder of one's interior psyche or from exterior demonic suggestion.[14] In fact, the Evil One and his minions prefer this interior mode of influence, since thoughts can corrupt the person and induce him to act. "Sin in regard to the intellect is easier than the sin in regard to act ... the mind is something easily moved and hard to restrain from unlawful fantasies."[15]

Evagrius focuses upon eight principal thoughts or temptations that follow an ascending order of gravity: the physical thoughts of gluttony and lust; the interior temptations of avarice, grief, anger, and acedia; and, finally, the crowning evils of vainglory and pride.[16] All these temptations enkindle the passions, disturb the psychological balance, and potentially move one to

12. *In Matthaeum* 19, 282–83, in Prevost, *Matthew*, 298–99.
13. Evagrius Ponticus, *Praktikos* (*Traité Pratique*) 74, ed. A Guillaumont and C. Guillaumont, SC 171 (Paris: Cerf, 1971), 662, lines 1–2.
14. See Evagrius, *Praktikos* 34, SC 171, 578, lines 1–6.
15. Evagrius, *Praktikos* 48, SC 171, 608, lines 5–8.
16. Evagrius, *Praktikos* 6, SC 171, 506, lines 1–2; 508, lines 3–8.

sinful action. The demons therefore use these thoughts to make persons more like themselves—that is, creatures that have abandoned the governing principle of reason (*logos*) in favor of the reigning forces of wrath (*thumos*) and disordered appetite (*epithumia*).

Yet, temptations in and of themselves have no power if one refuses to embrace them and act on them. Thoughts, Evagrius notes, will come throughout our lifetime, but in the end, it is what we *do with them* that counts. In fact, he defines sin as "*the consent* to a forbidden pleasure that comes from a thought."[17] One cannot avoid temptations, since they will always present themselves to our fallen minds. Yet, we also have the capacity, elevated by grace, to resist their power.

How, exactly, do we respond to temptations? Evagrius offers much advice in his extant works, but the following themes stand out. First, one must make a regular examen and discern the different kinds of temptations that enter one's mind. "It is necessary to know the differences among the demons and to mark the times of their coming."[18] In short, if one recognizes the kinds of enemies and their frequency, one can better prepare to meet them.

Second, one should apply spiritual exercises—the Greek *askēsis*—in order to strengthen the mind and will against temptations. Fasting, vigils, and other penances in due moderation give one greater discipline before the onslaught of the Evil One. Though the monks demonstrate these practices in a radical way, all Christians must follow certain disciplines of mind and body in the face of temptations.

Finally, one must turn to prayer, since divine aid is essential for victory over temptations. In particular, God's Word offers the weapons for spiritual defense. Evagrius composed a remarkable work consisting of short scriptural passages that one can memo-

17. Evagrius, *Praktikos* 75, SC 171, 662, lines 3–4.
18. Evagrius, *Praktikos* 43, SC 171, 598, lines 1–2.

rize and use as responses to various thoughts. His *Antirrhētikos*—the "Talking Back" book—therefore uses the model of Jesus in the desert by providing sacred words to interiorly "yell back" at attacking demons.[19] Spiritual combat demands our personal discipline, but in the end it is our reliance on God's gifts—God's Word and grace—that will win the day.

God Allows Temptations and Trials for a Time

This recognition of the devil's influence in no way implies a form of dualism—that is, the existence of two equal powers, Good and Evil, in conflict. On the contrary, Cyprian points out that the petition confirms the Adversary's lack of genuine power over humanity: "We are shown in this clause that the adversary can do nothing against us unless God allows it beforehand. Thus, all our fear and our devotion and heedfulness should be directed toward God, so that when we are in temptation he allows no power to the Evil One apart from which he grants."[20] God always reigns supreme and will give the necessary aid to overcome the enticements of the devil. Origen writes, "For when we have done all that is in our power, God will make up whatever is lacking through our human weakness as he works together with those who love him for good in all things (Rom 8:28), since in accordance with his inerrant foreknowledge he has foreseen what they shall come to be."[21]

But if God is omnipotent, why does he allow such trials? Two reasons come to the fore. First, God permits temptations and testing in order that sinfulness may become manifest. The postlapsarian ignorance in the human intellect often obfuscates the presence of personal and communal faults. Temptation, how-

---

19. For the English translation, see Evagrius of Pontus, *Talking Back: A Monastic Handbook for Combating Demons*, trans. David Brakke (Collegeville, Minn.: Cistercian, 2009).

20. *De oratione dom.* 25, PL 4, 536C, in Stewart-Sykes, *Lord's Prayer*, 84.

21. *De or.* 29, 19, PG 11, 545B, in Stewart-Sykes, *Lord's Prayer*, 204.

ever, drives such weaknesses into the open and forces man to seek healing for his wounds. Origen summarizes this process:

The utility of testing is thus something like this: through testing the things which our souls have admitted, unknown to anyone except God, unknown even to ourselves, are made manifest, so that we should no longer be unaware of what kind of people we are, but may recognize this and, should we so wish, perceive our own evil and give thanks for the good things which have been made manifest to us through the testing.[22]

God therefore *allows* temptations as a propaedeutic instrument. The nature of the trials often reflects the degree of sinfulness: the greater the presence of sin, the greater the trials produced from them. The suffering and struggles then expose corruption for all to see. "For power against us," writes Cyprian, "is given to the Evil One in proportion to our sins, as it is written, 'Who gave Jacob over to pillage and Israel to shoes who plundered him? Was it not God, against whom they sinned, refusing to walk in his ways or to hear his law? And he has poured out the rage of his provocation upon them'" (Is 42:25).[23]

Second, God allows trials in order that man may defeat sin and grow in virtue. At the heart of this position lies the Fathers' teaching of the inviolability of man's freedom. God desires that man *freely* choose divine life. Man's liberty therefore requires training in the struggle against temptation. Once again, Origen concisely summarizes this doctrine:

I do think that God deals with each rational soul in such a way as to lead it to eternal life, though it always possesses free will and on its own account may ascend to the summit of goodness through the better things, or may otherwise descend to a certain degree on account of heedlessness to the extent of wickedness. Accordingly, since a speedy and rapid cure may bring about contempt in some people for the dis-

22. *De or.* 29, 17, PG 11, 544B, in Stewart-Sykes, *Lord's Prayer*, 203.
23. *De oratione dom.* 25, PL 4, 537A, in Stewart-Sykes, *Lord's Prayer*, 84.

ease into which they have fallen ... so he may, in such cases, reasonably allow the evil to increase, allowing it so to augment within them as to be incurable, so that wallowing in the evil for a long time and being surfeited with the sin after which they longed, they may be sated and be made aware of the harm they have done to themselves.[24]

Experiencing the full horror of the fall, man will redirect his will toward the principle of his nature. Maximus writes that "he [man] should safeguard by reason the nature which of itself is pure and spotless, without hatred or dissension. He should on the contrary make free will a partner of nature which does not involve itself in anything beyond what the principle of nature gives out."[25]

This does not mean, however, that the Fathers failed to consider the need for divine aid in the spiritual struggle. The petition itself teaches the need for divine assistance in resisting disordered attractions. Even defeats before the onslaught of the devil serve to humiliate man and turn him toward the true source of his strength. "One feels rather humble regarding himself and does not presume to be saved by his own strength when he begs to be freed through God from evil."[26] We pray that "we should not be engulfed by testing, for those who are in its midst are so overcome."[27]

Conclusion: Times of Temptation, Trial, and Hope

Have the Fathers, in responding to this *aporia*, justified the presence of temptation and trial in the world? Have they simply given suffering and the seductive power of evil a natural place in God's plan? This would be, of course, an abomination. Eric Perl notes this difficulty: "For to explain something is to show how it is in

---

24. *De or.* 29, 13, PL 11, 538D–39A, in Stewart-Sykes, *Lord's Prayer*, 199.
25. *Or. dom.*, CCG 23, 69, lines 740–46, in Berthold, *Maximus*, 117.
26. *Col. serm.* 68.10, CCL 24A, 410, lines 104–5.
27. *De or.* 28.11, PG 11, 536D, in Stewart-Sykes, *Lord's Prayer*, 197.

some way good.... This is why most 'theodicies' fail precisely insofar as they succeed. To the extent that they satisfactorily account for or make sense of evil, they tacitly or expressly deny that it is evil and show that it is in fact good."[28]

On the one hand, the Fathers do, in fact, find a place for temptations and evils in creation. Temptation and trials can teach humanity regarding its sinfulness and need for God; they can awaken humanity to the presence of evil and the need to combat demonic influence. The Fathers emphatically deny that God is the source of temptation, but they do teach that God will make use of the brokenness of creation to lead human beings back to himself.

On the other hand, the Fathers also preached that evil is *unnatural* and represents a deep, destructive scar in the cosmos. It is a parasite born of disordered wills that feeds on the Good. "Evil," writes Gregory of Nyssa, "subsists as soon as it is chosen; it comes into being whenever we elect it. It has no substance of its own."[29] Our response must therefore be one of outrage toward evil and the Evil One. Evagrius Ponticus teaches that one uses anger in a positive way by directing it toward evil itself: "The nature of anger (*thumos*) is to fight demons and to struggle against every [disordered] pleasure."[30] Evil and suffering deserve our condemnation, even while we must recognize such things as our condign punishment for our disordered choices.

In turn, the experience of trial and temptation finds its ultimate response not in a formula, but in a person: the suffering Son on the cross. Suffering finds redemptive meaning in the Son, and therefore "to be led into temptation/trial" is actually a deeper participation in the redemptive power of the cross. The Master wrote, "When Christ provided for us the refuge of his cross, the Lord destroyed the sting of death which was reigning over us. Af-

28. Eric Perl, *Theophany: The Neoplatonic Philosophy of Dionysius the Areopagite* (New York: State University of New York Press, 2007), 63–64.

29. *Beat.* 5, GNO 7.2, 129, lines 19–22, in Graef, *Lord's Prayer*, 135–36.

30. Evagrius, *Praktikos*, SC 171, 556, lines 1–2.

ter restoring us to the grace of adoption by him, he has moreover not ceased to invite us to the kingdom of heaven.... Therefore, it behooves us to share in his sufferings so that we may deserve to be made coheirs of his glory."[31] John Paul II made this point in his apostolic letter *Salvifici doloris*: "Christ does not explain in the abstract the reasons for suffering, but before all else he says, 'Follow me!' Come! Take part through your suffering in this work of saving the world."[32]

There will, however, come a time in which all temptations will cease and the devil will experience total defeat. God may allow trials, but God's providence will not permit them to endure. The "deliverance from evil" expresses the great hope of humanity: the fulfillment of Christ's victory in history. To seek deliverance in this life is presumptuous, but to live in the hope of this liberation in the consummation of history sustains humanity in the journey. Augustine conveys this great hope to his audience:

> But we must also pray to be delivered from the evil into which we have been already led. When the deliverance is accomplished, nothing will remain to be dreaded, and then there will be no need to fear any temptation whatever. There is not ground for hope that this can be brought about in our present life, for it cannot come to pass as long as we are carrying about with us the mortality to which we have been brought by the enticement of the serpent. However, we must hope that it will come to pass sometime; this is the hope that is not seen, the hope of which the Apostle was speaking, when he said: "But the hope that is seen, is not hope" (Rom 8:24).[33]

"Deliver us, Lord, from every evil." This cry for deliverance is also an act of hope toward a God who suffered that all might be saved and rejoice.

---

31. *Regula*, SC 105, 302, lines 68–76, in Eberle, *Rule*, 96.
32. John Paul II, Apostolic Letter *Salvifici doloris* (February 11, 1984), 26.
33. *De serm. Dom.* II.9.35, CCL 25, 125, lines 762–71, in Kavanagh, *Commentary*, 143–44.

CONCLUSION

I now return to the commentary known as the ROTAS-SATOR square. It depicts the Lord's Prayer in the form of the cross, and it is framed by the *alpha-omega*. The prayer is therefore the itinerary of the Christian journey, the formation of the person from the beginning (*alpha*) to the end (*omega*) in the light of the cross. The mysteries of the Lord's Prayer and the Fathers' responses provide the basic elements of this journey.

1. Divine adoption   This is the *alpha*. The Christian is reborn in baptism and acquires the full right to call God "Father." He or she now has the mission to live up to the name by following the One who is Son by nature: Jesus Christ.

2. Pilgrimage   The Christian now sees his or her life as a pilgrimage to the true home in the household of the Father. Heaven contains the heart's treasure—union with the Father—and becomes the determining goal for every Christian pilgrim.

3. The Greater Glory of God   *Ad maiorem Dei gloriam*. God's name is absolutely holy. Nothing can add or subtract from this glory. Yet, the Christian glorifies God in himself and in the world through word, action, and worship. God's holiness then becomes manifest in the Christian community and draws others toward the Lord.

4. Citizen of/in the kingdom   The Christian is a citizen of heaven while living on earth. On the one hand, he or she is not *of* the world and can find no genuine fulfillment in it: only God

can bring about the kingdom. On other hand, the Christian lives *in* the world and therefore works to demonstrate the reality of God's loving rule even in this passing age. The *now* and *not yet* are the marks of the divine reign; the presence and anticipation of the kingdom dynamize every Christian's life.

5. Conformity to the divine will The human will, perverted by a primordial act of disobedience, requires a re-formation through the person of Jesus Christ. The God-Man accepted the cup of suffering and redirected the human will toward the Father. The Christian finds fulfillment in conforming his will with the Father's through obedience to the divine commands and the acceptance of a divinely given mission.

6. The Bread of Life The Christian separates himself from false goods and disordered desires in order to live a life of simplicity. In such a life the Christian finds sustenance in the reception of the Bread of Life: Jesus Christ. The Eucharist is his true daily bread.

7. Forgiveness The Christian forgives because he or she has been forgiven through the blood of Christ. Living in a world of debts, the debtor—every human person mired in sin—reflects the divine remission of sins through the practice of forgiveness.

8. Sharing in the suffering of Christ The Son of God became man and shared fallen humanity's trials. His suffering revealed fully his divinity and the depths of his love. Temptations and trials therefore become redemptive when united with Christ on the cross. The Christian prays, "Lead us not into trial/temptation," but with the *coda* pronounced by the Son in Gethsemane: "Not my will, but yours be done."

9. Hope This is the *omega*. Hope is not a wish. Hope grounds itself in the possible and in the promises of One who does not lie. "Deliver us from evil." Christ has promised to deliver us from suffering and death and to bring us into the household of the Father. The Lord's Prayer concludes with an affirmation of this greatest

hope that inspires every Christian in the pilgrimage. Thus, the Master concludes his commentary in these words: "Thus may he, who at the beginning of the prayer shows us that we should dare, by his grace, to call the lord our Father, deign now at the end of the prayer to deliver us from evil. Amen."[1]

The *Didache's* version of the Lord's Prayer ends with a doxology, a proclamation of God's glory: "Because yours is the power and the glory forever." The Christian who, by God's grace, comes to the end of this pilgrimage does indeed glorify God. Jesus told his followers "to pray like this"—that is, to pray and live this wondrous compendium of the Gospel that leads to everlasting life. *Because yours is the power and the glory forever!*

1. *Regula*, SC 105, 316, lines 221–23, in Eberle, *Rule*, 101.

APPENDIX: BRIEF PORTRAITS OF THE FATHERS

Augustine of Hippo (354–430)

Augustine remains a giant in the history of Latin Christianity and culture. His remarkable and moving conversion story, recounted in *The Confessions*, traces his life from his birth in the Roman province of Numidia, through his tumultuous youth, to his reversion to Christian orthodoxy. His long life truly entered the public stage with his ascendency to the episcopacy of Hippo, in North Africa, in 395. Over a period of nearly four decades he engaged in controversy, taught and guided his flock, and composed masterworks in theology, scriptural commentary, and spirituality. We fortunately possess several reflections on the Lord's Prayer in his homilies and the Letter to Proba.

Chromatius of Aquileia (d. 406)

Little is known about the life of Chromatius, who was born in the Roman city of Aquileia and became the bishop of the city in the late fourth century. He actively opposed Arianism and corresponded with such contemporary luminaries as Jerome, John Chrysostom, and Rufinus. His comments on the Lord's Prayer appear in his writings on the Gospel of Matthew.

Cyprian of Carthage (210–58)

Born to a wealthy family in Carthage, Cyprian converted to Christianity in his mid-thirties. He later received orders and became bishop of Carthage around 249. He survived the great persecution of Emperor Decius by going into hiding, but upon his return he had to confront the controversies surrounding the readmission of lapsed Christians. He became a martyr during the renewed persecution under Emperor Valerian. His writings deal especially with problems surrounding the Church's identity and the sacraments. Even his *On the Lord's Prayer*, one of the earliest treatments of the prayer, emphasizes the unity of the Church.

Cyril of Jerusalem (315?–86)

We know little about the early life of Cyril. He became bishop of Jerusalem around 350. His defense of the Council of Nicaea and other political issues drew the ire of powerful enemies, and he suffered through several periods of exile from his see. His catechetical lectures provide a glimpse into the liturgical practices and theology in the Eastern Church of the mid-fourth century. His comments on the Lord's Prayer appear within his treatment of the Eucharistic liturgy.

Evagrius Ponticus (345–99)

Evagrius grew up in a Christian family in what is now Turkey. He later became a lector under Basil the Great and a deacon under Gregory of Nazianzus. He accompanied Gregory to Constantinople when the latter became, for a brief period, the capital's patriarch. After Gregory's departure, Evagrius remained to enjoy the extravagances that the city offered. Finally awakened to the dangers of his sensuous lifestyle, he departed first for Jerusalem and then for the Egyptian desert in order to live in the manner of the renowned ascetics in the region. His masterful treatises on monastic spirituality became widespread and influential. Versions of a brief commentary on the Lord's Prayer survive in a Syriac translation.

Gregory of Nyssa (335–95)

Gregory of Nyssa was the true mystic among the great Cappadocian Fathers, whose number includes Basil the Great and Gregory of Nazianzus. He received a superb education from his sister, Macrina, and spent a short period as a professional rhetorician. Through the influence of Basil the Great, who was his brother, he became bishop of Nyssa in 372. He was active in the doctrinal debates of his day, especially those surrounding the Trinity, and was a participant in the Council of Constantinople in 381. His writings, which include *Homilies on the Lord's Prayer* and *Homilies on the Beatitudes*, continue to impress readers with their speculative range and profound spiritual insights.

Jerome of Stridon (347–420)

The patron of biblical scholars, Jerome was born in Stridon, in the province of Dalmatia. While a student in Rome he engaged in various youthful excesses, but his life took a radical turn after his conversion and baptism in the mid-360s. After a journey through Asia Minor and encounters with the great ascetics of the desert, Jerome embarked on the ascetic life and was ordained in Antioch in 378. His prodigious learning—he could read Latin, Greek, and Hebrew—brought him to the attention of Pope Damasus, who made Jerome his secretary and commissioned him to prepare a new version of the Latin Bible. He would eventually leave Rome and settle in a cave in Bethlehem, surrounded by disciples—especially a group of influential women from Rome—who shared his vision for a monastic and scholarly community. In addition to his work of translation, Jerome also composed Scripture commentaries, monastic lives, theological writings, and numerous letters. His writings on the Lord's Prayer appear in his *Commentary on the Gospel of Matthew.*

John Cassian (360–435)

The birthplace of John Cassian remains unknown, though some scholars point toward the region of modern Romania. As a young man he spent time in a monastery in Bethlehem and later came to know the monks of Egypt. His time with the legendary ascetics gave him a rich supply of wisdom regarding the Christian pursuit of holiness. After some years of controversy and travel, he accepted an invitation to found a monastery in Marseilles. He successfully imported many of the practices and structures he had encountered in Egypt, along with his own modifications for Western living. His *Conferences*, which consist of a series of conversations with famed Egyptian ascetics on a variety of topics, and his *Institutes* influenced many Western monks, including Benedict of Nursia. The Ninth Conference provides an explanation and application of the Lord's Prayer.

John Chrysostom (349–407)

John "the Golden-mouthed" was born in the Syrian city of Antioch and received rhetorical training from the renowned pagan teacher Libanius. He spent two years as a hermit and dedicated himself intensely to the study of the Scriptures. He was then ordained a deacon in 381 and a priest in 386. In the subsequent years his reputation as a preacher and defender of the poor spread far and wide. In 397 he became the patriarch of Constantinople. Though bishop of the capital, he lived an ascetic lifestyle and openly defended the poor and downtrodden, thereby often provoking the ire of the elite class. Jealousies and political machinations motivated powerful figures to form a conspiracy against the saintly preacher, and a synod of his enemies exiled John from his see in 403. He died in exile in 407. His published homilies and treatises, and his reputation for sanctity established him as one of the most beloved Christian figures of antiquity. His insights on the Lord's Prayer may be found in his *Homilies on the Gospel of Matthew.*

The Master (dates unknown)

The Rule of the Master (*Regula Magistri*) is a collection of monastic rules and counsels from the sixth century. It influenced Benedict of Nursia and other monastic founders. The treatment of the Lord's Prayer establishes one of the themes of the work: the Fatherhood of God and the brotherhood established in the community.

Maximus the Confessor (580–662)

Extant lives of Maximus conflict regarding the origins of this great ascetic, theologian, and martyr. One account maintains that Maximus was an official in the court of Emperor Heraclius and that he gave up his prestigious career to become a monk. He was forced to flee his monastery on the Bosporus when the Persians invaded, and he spent time in the North African monastery of Sophronius, the future patriarch of Jerusalem. His prodigious learning made him a powerful defender of orthodoxy during the monothelite controversy (the debate regarding the number of Christ's wills), and he traveled to Rome in 649 to participate in the Lateran Council. He and Pope Martin I rejected the emperor's demands to affirm monothelitism, and they defended the two wills of Christ at the cost of their lives: Pope Martin died after torture and imprisonment; Maximus died in exile after having his tongue cut out and his right hand cut off. His dense and complicated writings are some of the most sublime contributions to Christian theology and spirituality from the ancient world. His short *Commentary on the Lord's Prayer* offers priceless treasures to the diligent reader.

Origen of Alexandria (184–253)

Origen remains one of the most influential and controversial theologians of Christianity. The son of a martyr, Leonides, Origen received an exceptional formation in the commercial and intellectual hub of Alexandria. His later work as a teacher and Christian philosopher brought him both renown and, at times, condemnation from bishops and laity alike. His writings include Scripture commentaries, apologetics such as the *Against Celsus*, the great work of speculative and systematic theology called *On First Principles*, and other writings of tremendous spiritual value. He spent his later life in Caeserea and died after being released from a brutal two-year imprisonment during a persecution under Emperor Decius. His reflections on the Lord's Prayer appear in his *On Prayer (De oratione)*.

Peter Chrysologus (380–450)

Peter "the Golden-word" was born and raised in Imola, near Bologna. He became bishop of Ravenna in 433. The city, an important bridge between the Eastern and Western Churches, was still struggling with Arianism and the more recent heresy of monophysitism—the heresy that Christ had only one nature. Peter responded to the controversies with his elegant, profound, and comparatively brief homilies, which both educated and edified the faithful. Several of his extant sermons treat the words of the Lord's Prayer.

Tertullian (155–240)

Tertullian has often received the title of "the Father of Latin Christianity." Born in Carthage, he was a trained rhetor and bilingual (Latin and Greek) scholar who converted to Christianity in his early forties. His extant writings traverse such subjects as apologetics (*The Apologeticus, On Idolatry, Against Praxeas*, etc.), theology (*On the Flesh of Christ, On the Resurrection of Christ*, etc.) and Christian living (*An Exhortation to Chastity, On Monogamy, On Fasting*, etc.). Though his later association with the Christian sect known as Montanism has made him suspect to many, his writings nonetheless influenced generations of Christians. His treatment of the Lord's Prayer appears in his *On Prayer* (*De oratione*).

Theodore of Mopsuestia (350–428)

Theodore was born to a family of means in Antioch. In his late teens he became part of a circle of ascetics that included John Chrysostom. However, he abandoned this life for a time to pursue a career as a lawyer and to seek marriage. John Chrysostom, in two letters that remain to us, sought to persuade his younger friend to return to monasticism. The great preacher was evidently successful, since Theodore did return and around 392 became bishop of Mopsuestia in Cilicia. He was a greatly admired preacher and teacher in his own lifetime, though elements of his theology would be condemned by later generations. His *Catechetical Homilies* survive in Syriac translations: one homily on the Creed and another on the Lord's Prayer.

BIBLIOGRAPHY

Christian Primary Sources

The bibliography that follows contains all the patristic sources cited in this volume, including those works that do not treat the Lord's Prayer. For authors not included in the appendix, I have included their birth and death years. For each work I provide some brief comments, an available English translation, and the Greek or Latin text consulted in this work; series are abbreviated according to the list on pp. xxi–xxii. As noted in the introduction, this volume provides a synthesis of modern and ancient wisdom in order to answer some *aporiai* posed by the Fathers. Yet, it should not be forgotten that each Father has his own approach to the Lord's Prayer and the mysteries within. It is my hope that the reader will make use of the following bibliography and read the original works—the true sources of ancient wisdom and holiness.

Augustine of Hippo

The Confessions (c. 397–400): In this, the best known of Augustine's works, the reader follows the odyssey of a restless heart that finds peace in God. It is a work of prayer that inspires the reader to follow Augustine's path to the joyful praise of the Lord. Latin: *Augustine: Confessions.* Vol. 1. Edited by James O'Donnell. Oxford: Oxford University Press, 2012. English: *The Confessions.* Translated by Maria Boulding, OSB. New York: New City Press, 1997.

Letter 130 (*Letter to Proba*, c. 412): In this letter to Anicia Faltonia Proba, a wealthy Roman widow who sought Augustine's advice on how to pray, Augustine offers sage advice on the spiritual life, including a practical commentary on the Lord's Prayer. Latin: *Epistula 130*. In *Epistulae*. PL 33, 493–507. English: "Letter 130." In *Letters 100–155*, translated by Roland Teske, SJ, 183–89. New York: New City Press, 2003.

On the Sermon on the Mount (c. 393): This work was Augustine's first commentary dealing with a New Testament text. A young priest at the time of composition, Augustine treats the Sermon on the Mount as a spiritual ascent that requires prayer and asceticism. Latin: *De sermone Domini in monte*. Edited by Almut Mutzenbecher. CCL 35. Turnhout: Brepols, 1967. English: *On the Sermon on the Mount*. In *Commentary on the Lord's Sermon on the Mount with Seventeen Related Sermons*, translated by Denis Kavanagh, OSA, 19–197. Washington, D.C.: The Catholic University of America Press, 1951.

On the Trinity (399–422): This remarkable work on trinitarian theology, composed by Augustine over an extended period, has influenced generations of Christian theologians. It is a compelling work of scriptural exegesis and theological speculation. Latin: *De Trinitate*. Edited by W. J. Mountain and F. Glorie. CCL 50/50A. Turnhout: Brepols, 1968. English: *The Trinity*. Translated by Edmund Hill, OP. New York: New City Press, 1991.

Sermons 56–59 (c. 410–15): Augustine preached these sermons to those preparing for baptism. Each one includes an exposition on the Lord's Prayer. Latin: *Sermones 56–59*. In *Sermones*. PL 38, 377–402. English: "Sermons 56–59." In *Sermons 51–94*, translated by Edmund Hill, OP, 95–131. New York: New City Press, 1991.

Chromatius of Aquileia

Sermons and Tractates on Matthew (c. 400–405): Little was known about Chromatius's works until texts—many of which had been copied under the names of other authors—were published in the 1960s. His commentary on the Lord's Prayer comes from his sermons on Matthew's Gospel. Latin and French: *Chromace D'Aquilée*. Edited by Joseph Lemarié. SC 154. Paris: Cerf, 1971. English: *Chromatius of Aquileia: Sermons and Tractates on Matthew*. Translated by Thomas Scheck. Melville, N.Y.: Ambassador, 2018.

Clement of Alexandria (150–215)

Stromateis: Clement, a Christian convert, was a theologian, philosopher, and head of the catechetical school in Alexandria. The *Stromateis*, or "Carpet Weavings," treats a variety of theological and philosophical topics. Note: The work does not contain a commentary on the Lord's Prayer. Greek and French: *Stromate VII.* Edited by Alain le Boulluec. SC 428. Paris: Cerf, 1997. English: *The Stromata.* In *The Ante-Nicene Fathers*, vol. 2, *The Fathers of the Second Century*, edited by A. Cleveland Coxe, 299–568. New York: Christian Literature, 1885.

Cyprian of Carthage

On the Lord's Prayer (c. 251–52): Cyprian knew Tertullian's work on the Lord's Prayer, though he offers a much more extensive treatment and even comments on a slightly different version of the Prayer. Latin: *De oratione dominica.* PL 4, 519–44. English: "On the Lord's Prayer." In *On the Lord's Prayer: Tertullian, Cyprian and Origen on the Lord's Prayer*, translated by Alistair Stewart-Sykes, 65–93. Crestwood, N.Y.: St. Vladimir's Seminary Press, 2004.

Cyril of Jerusalem

Mystagogical Catechesis (c. 348): Cyril gave these lectures before becoming bishop of Jerusalem in 351. The five discourses address the recently baptized. It includes a treatment of the Lord's Prayer. Greek: *Catecheses mystagogicae quinque.* PG 33, 1065–1128. English: *Lectures on the Christian Sacraments.* Translated by F. L. Cross. Crestwood, N.Y.: St. Vladimir's Press, 1995.

The Didache

The Didache (late first century). This is an invaluable work that gives us a glimpse into the formation and practices of the early Christians, including instructions on how to pray a version of the Lord's Prayer. Greek and English: *The Didache: Faith, Hope, and Life of the Earliest Christian Communities 50–70 C.E.* Edited by Aaron Milavec. New York: Newman Press, 2003.

Evagrius of Pontus

Our Father (late fourth century): Only fragments of this work survive in Coptic and Arabic. English: "Our Father." In *Evagrius Ponticus*, translated by A. M. Casiday, 150–52. New York: Routledge, 2006.

Antirrhetikos (late fourth century): This work offers a collection of scriptural verses that can be used for "talking back" to demons and the temptations toward various vices. The complete text survives in Syriac and Armenian. English: *Talking Back: A Monastic Handbook for Combating Demons*. Translated by David Brakke. Collegeville, Minn.: Cistercian, 2009.

The Praktikos (late fourth century): In this work Evagrius provides monks with a guide to the ascetical life and the purgation of vices. Greek and French: *Traité Pratique*. Edited by A Guillaumont and C. Guillaumont. SC 171. Paris: Cerf, 1971. English: "A Treatise on the Practical Life." In *The Greek Ascetic Corpus*, translated by Robert E. Sinkewicz, 95–114. Oxford: Oxford University Press, 2003.

Gregory of Nazianzus

Discourses 27–31, or *"The Five Theological Orations"* (c. 379–81): He composed these discourses during his brief and tumultuous period in Constantinople. Together these orations offer a summary and synthesis of the Cappadocian response to the trinitarian debates of the fourth century. Greek and French: *Discours 27–31*. Edited by P. Gallay. SC 250. Paris: Cerf, 1978. English: *On God and Christ: The Five Theological Orations and the Letters to Cledonius*. Edited by John Behr. New York: St. Vladimir's Seminary Press, 2011.

Gregory of Nyssa

On the Beatitudes (c. 378): This series of homilies instruct Christians on how to make a spiritual ascent through prayer and ascetical practice. Greek: *De Beatitudinibus*. In *De oratione dominica: De beatitudinibus*, edited by J. Callahan, 75–170. GNO 7.2. New York: Brill, 1992. English: "On the Beatitudes." In *The Lord's Prayer and the Beatitudes*, translated by Hilda Graef, 85–175. New York: Paulist Press, 1954.

On the Lord's Prayer (c. 375): Gregory, known primarily as a mystic and a highly speculative thinker, in this case gave a series of practical and inspiring homilies in order to help his congregation live an authentic Christian life. Together they stand out as one of the most beautiful commentaries on the Lord's Prayer ever composed. Greek: *De oratione dominica*. In *De oratione dominica: De beatiutdinibus*, edited by J. Callahan, 1–74. GNO 7.2. New York: Brill, 1992. English: "On the Lord's Prayer." In *The Lord's Prayer and the Beatitudes*, translated by Hilda Graef, 21–84. New York: Paulist Press, 1954.

On the Making of Man (c. 379): Gregory wrote this work to fill a lacuna in his brother Basil's commentary on the Hexameron (the six days of creation in the *Book of Genesis*). Greek: *De hominis opificio*. PG 44, 123–256. English: "On the Making of Man." In *Nicene and Post-Nicene Fathers*, vol. 5, *Gregory of Nyssa*, translated by W. Moore and H. A. Wilson, 387–427. New York: Christian Literature, 1893.

On Virginity (c. 370): This work, the earliest of Gregory's ascetical writings, extols virginity as the foundation of the virtues and a form of spiritual marriage to the Bridegroom Christ. Greek: *De virginibus*. Edited by J. P. Cavaronos. GNO 8. Leiden: Brill, 1952. English: "On Virginity." In *Nicene and Post-Nicene Fathers*, vol. 5, *Gregory of Nyssa*, translated by W. Moore and H. A. Wilson, 343–71. New York: Christian Literature, 1893.

Irenaeus of Lyon (130–202)

Against the Heresies V (late second century): Irenaeus, the bishop of Lyon, confronted the teachings of various gnostic groups in this major contribution to early Christian apologetics and theology. Note: It does not contain a dedicated treatment on the Lord's Prayer. Greek and French: *Contre les Hérésies V*. Edited by Adelin Rousseau. SC 153. Paris: Cerf, 1969. English: *Against Heresies*. In *The Ante-Nicene Fathers*, vol. 2, *The Fathers of the Second Century*, edited by A. Cleveland Coxe, 309–567. New York: Christian Literature, 1885.

Jerome of Stridon

On Matthew (c. 398): Although Jerome depends greatly on Origen's commentary on Matthew, nonetheless he does offer significant original insights, including his treatment of the Lord's Prayer. Latin and French:

Commentaire sur S. Matthieu I. Edited by Émile Bonnard. SC 242. Paris: Cerf, 1977. English: *Commentary on Matthew.* Translated by Thomas Scheck. Washington, D.C: The Catholic University of America Press, 2014.

John Cassian

Conferences (c. 425–29): John Cassian brought the wisdom of the eastern desert fathers to the West through this collection of treatises. Each conference allows a particular desert father (Daniel, Theodore, Serenus, and others) to speak on a topic of the Christian ascetical life. In "Conference IX," Abba Isaac discusses prayer, including an explanation of the Lord's Prayer. Latin: *Collationes.* PL 49:481–1328. English: John Cassian. *The Conferences.* Translated by Boniface Ramsey, OP. New York: Newman Press, 1997.

John Chrysostom

Homilies on Matthew (c. 390): John Chrysostom gave these homilies in Antioch. They contain not only practical spiritual advice for his congregation, but also important theological treatments of trinitarian theology and Christology. "Homily 19" contains his treatment of the Lord's Prayer. Greek: *Homiliae in Matthaeum.* Vol. 1. Edited by Fridericus Field. Cambridge: Officina Academica, 1839. English: *The Homilies of St. John Chrysostom on the Gospel of Matthew.* Translated S. G. Prevost. Oxford: J. H. Parker, 1843.

Macarius of Egypt (300–391)

This legendary ascetic of the Egyptian desert guided disciples in the growth in virtues and the spiritual life. His surviving homilies continue to inspire Christians in both the East and West. Note: They do not contain a dedicated treatment of the Lord's Prayer. Greek: *Homiliae.* PG 34, 449–820. English: *The Fifty Spiritual Homilies and the Great Letter.* Translated by George Maloney, SJ. Mahwah, N.J.: Paulist Press, 1992.

The Master

Regula Magistri (c. 520–30): The unknown author of this monastic rule influenced the more well-known rule of St. Benedict. The author discusses the Lord's Prayer within a treatment of spiritual sonship at the very beginning of the Rule. French: *La Régle du Maître*. Edited by Adalbert de Vogüé. SC 105. Paris: Cerf, 1964. English: *The Rule of the Master*. Translated by Luke Eberle, OSB. Collegeville, Minn.: Cistercian, 1977.

Maximus the Confessor

The Ambigua to John (c. 628): This collection addresses a series of questions dealing primarily with the works of Gregory of Nazianzus. Greek and English Text: *On Difficulties in the Church Fathers. The "Ambigua."* Vols. 1–2. Edited and translated by Nicholas Constas. Cambridge, Mass.: Harvard University Press, 2014.

On the Lord's Prayer (c. 636): Maximus's commentary on the Lord's Prayer can prove challenging for the reader. It is, by far, the most speculative of the commentaries discussed in this book. Yet, it also offers some of the most profound insights on prayer and the spiritual life that come to us from early eastern Christianity. Greek: *Expositio orationis dominicae*. Edited by P. Van Deun. CCG 23. Turnhout: Brepols, 1991. English: In *Maximus the Confessor: Selected Writings*, translated by George Berthold, 99–125. New York: Paulist Press, 1985.

Opuscula theologica et polemica 1 (c. 645): A short work that is found in a collection of Maximus's responses to theological questions. Greek: PG 91, 28B–39C.

Origen of Alexandria

Against Celsus (c. 246): Origen's friend Ambrose asked him to respond to a work that had been written by Celsus, a highly educated philosopher, in 178. Celsus had mounted a powerful argument against the Christians, and it took Origen's considerable talents to answer the charges. Greek and French: *Contre Celse*. Edited by Marcel Borret, SJ. SC 132, 136, 147, 150, 227. Paris: Cerf, 1968–76. English: *Contra Celsum*. Translated by Henry Chadwick. New York: Cambridge University Press, 1953.

Commentary on the Psalms (c. 220): The surviving excerpt comes to us through the "Philokalia," a collection of Origen's spiritual writings compiled by Basil the Great and Gregory of Nazianzus. Greek and

French: "Passages from 'Commentary on the Psalms.'" In *Philocalie, 1–20: Sur les Écritures,* edited by Marguerite Harl, SC 302, 245–49. English: "Commentary on the Psalms." In *Origen,* translated by Joseph Trigg, 71–72. New York: Routledge, 1998.

On Prayer (c. 233): Origen wrote this work for his friends Ambrose and Tatiana. Origen defines prayer, discusses the value and different types of prayer, and gives a remarkable commentary on the Our Father. Greek: *De oratione.* PG 11, 474–550. English: "On Prayer." In *On the Lord's Prayer,* translated by Alistair Stewart-Sykes, 95–214. Crestwood, N.Y.: St. Vladimir's Seminary Press, 2004.

Peter Chrysologus

Sermons 67–72 (mid-fifth century): Peter Chrysologus's homilies remain remarkably accessible to the modern reader: clear, concise, and full of insights and striking rhetorical flourishes. These homilies all treat the Lord's Prayer. Latin: *Collectio sermonum 67–72.* Edited by Alexander Olivar. CCL 24A. Turnhout: Brepols, 1981. English: "Sermons 68–72." In *Peter Chrysologus: Selected Sermons,* translated by William Palardy, 2:274–96. Washington, D.C.: The Catholic University of America Press, 2004.

Pseudo-Dionysius the Areopagite

The Divine Names (c. late fifth century): The work of this mysterious writer, who assumed the name of the Dionysius mentioned in *The Acts of the Apostles* 17:34, brought a form of late ancient neo-Platonism into the Christian world and had a tremendous influence on theological reflection in both the East and West. Note: This work does not contain a treatment of the Lord's Prayer. Greek: *Corpus Dionysiacum* I: *De Divinis Nominibus.* Edited by B. R. Suchla. PTS 33. Berlin: De Gruyter, 1990. English: "The Divine Names." In *Pseudo-Dionysius: The Complete Works,* translated by Colm Luibheid, 47–132. New York: Paulist Press, 1987.

Tertullian

On Prayer (c. 198–200): Addressed to Catechumens, this brief treatise contains the earliest complete exposition on the Lord's Prayer. Tertullian aims for the practical in this work, thereby providing important guidance for those new to the Christian faith. Latin: *De oratione*. PL 1, 1149–66. English: "On Prayer." In *On the Lord's Prayer*, translated by Alistair Stewart-Sykes, 41–64. Crestwood, N.Y.: St. Vladimir's Seminary Press, 2004.

Theodore of Mopsuestia

On the Lord's Prayer (c. 388–92): This forms part of Theodore's "Catechetical Homilies," which survive in a Syriac translation. They reveal the significance the Lord's Prayer for the formation of new Christians. English and Syriac: *Commentary of Theodore of Mopsuestia on the Lord's Prayer and the Sacraments of Baptism and the Eucharist*, translated by Alphonse Mingana, 1–16, 124–42. Piscataway, N.J.: Gorgias, 2009.

Secondary Sources

Albright, W. F., and C. S. Mann. *Matthew*: *Introduction, Translation, and Notes*. New York: Doubleday, 1971.

Anderson, Gary. *Sin*: *A History*. New Haven, Conn.: Yale University Press, 2009.

Bathrellos, Demetrios. *The Byzantine Christ*: *Person, Nature, and Will in the Christology of Saint Maximus the Confessor*. Oxford: Oxford University Press, 2004.

Benedict XVI. *Jesus of Nazareth*: *From the Baptism in the Jordan to the Transfiguration*. New York: Doubleday, 2007.

Bieler, Jonathan. "Maximus the Confessor on Christ's Human Will." *Communio* 43, no. 1 (Spring 2016): 58–66.

Black, C. Clifton. *The Lord's Prayer*. Louisville: Westminster John Knox Press, 2018.

Boersma, Hans. *Embodiment and Virtue in Gregory of Nyssa*: *An Analogical Approach*. Oxford: Oxford University Press, 2015.

Borg, Marcus. *Conflict, Holiness and Politics in the Teachings of Jesus*. Harrisburg, Pa.: Trinity Press International, 1998.

Boring, M. Eugene. *The Gospel of Matthew*. Nashville, Tenn.: Abingdon, 1995.

Brotherton, Joshua. "The 'Our Father' Translation Controversy." *Fellowship of Catholic Scholars Quarterly* 41, no. 3 (Fall 2018): 282–86.

Brown, Michael Joseph. "'*Panem Nostrum*': The Problem of Petition and the Lord's Prayer." *Journal of Religion* 80, no. 4 (2000): 595–613.

Brown, Raymond. "The *Pater Noster* as an Eschatological Prayer." In *New Testament Essays*, 175–208. New York: Paulist Press, 1968.

Carmignac, Jean. *Recherches sur le Notre Père*. Paris: Letouzey and Ane, 1969.

Crossan, John Dominic. *The Greatest Prayer: Rediscovering the Revolutionary Message of the "The Lord's Prayer."* New York: HarperCollins, 2010.

Culpepper, R. Alan. *Luke*. Nashville, Tenn.: Abingdon, 1995.

Davies, W. D., and D. C. Allison. *Matthew 1–7*. Vol. 1. New York: T. and T. Clark, 2004.

Day, C. "In Search of the Meaning of *Epiousios* in the Lord's Prayer: Rounding Up the Usual Suspects." *Acta Patristica et Byzantina* 14 (2003): 97–111.

de Lubac, Henri, SJ. *The Discovery of God*. Translated by Alexander Dru. Grand Rapids, Mich.: Eerdmans, 1996.

Doucet, M. "La volonté humaine du Christ, spécialement en son agonie: Maxime le Confesseur interprète de l'Écriture." *Science et Esprit* 37 (1985): 123–59.

Farley, Lawrence. *The Apocalypse of St. John: A Revelation of Love and Power*. Chesterton, Ind.: Conciliar Press, 2011.

Farrow, Douglas. *Ascension and Ecclesia*. Grand Rapids, Mich.: Eerdmans, 1999.

Fishwick, Duncan. "On the Origin of the Rotas-Sator Square." *Harvard Theological Review* 57, no. 1 (1964): 39–53.

Fitzmyer, Joseph. *The Gospel According to Luke X–XXIV*. New York: Paulist Press, 1985.

France, R. T. *The Gospel of Matthew*. Grand Rapids, Mich.: Eerdmans, 2007.

Gavin, John, SJ. *"They Are Like the Angels in the Heavens": Angelology and Anthropology in the Thought of Maximus the Confessor*. Rome: Studia Ephemeridis Augustinianum, 2009.

———. "Becoming an Exemplar for God: Three Early Interpretations of Forgiveness in the Lord's Prayer." *Logos* 16, no. 3 (2013): 126–46.

Gieschen, Charles. "The Divine Name in Ante-Nicene Christology." *Vigiliae Christianae* 57, no. 2 (2003): 115–58.

Grayston, Kenneth. "The Decline of Temptation and the Lord's Prayer." *Scottish Journal of Theology* 46, no. 3 (August 1993): 279–96.

Guardini, Romano. *The Lord's Prayer*. Translated by Isabel McHugh. New York: Pantheon, 1958.

Gundry, Robert. *Matthew: A Commentary on his Handbook for a Mixed Church under Persecution*. Grand Rapids, Mich.: Eerdmans, 1994.

Hammerling, Roy. "Gregory of Nyssa's Sermons on the Lord's Prayer: Lessons from the Classics." *Word and World* 22, no. 1 (2002): 64–70.

———. "The Lord's Prayer: A Cornerstone of Early Baptismal Education." In *A History of Prayer: The First to the Fifteenth Century*, edited by Roy Hammerling, 167–82. Leiden: Brill, 2008.

———. *The Lord's Prayer in the Early Church: The Pearl of Great Price*. New York: Palgrave Macmillan, 2010.

Harrington, Daniel, SJ. *The Gospel of Matthew*. Collegeville, Minn..: Liturgical Press, 2007.

Harvey, Anthony. "Daily Bread." *Theological Studies* 69 (April 2018): 25–38.

Howse, Christopher. "Unique Ancient Sator-Rotas Word-Square Discovered." *Telegraph*, May 2, 2015. http://www.telegraph.co.uk/comment/11579586/Unique-ancient-Sator-Rotas-word-square-discovered.html.

Hurtado, Larry. *Lord Jesus Christ: Devotion to Jesus in Earliest Christianity*. Grand Rapids, Mich.: Eerdmans, 2003.

Jeremias, Joachim. *The Lord's Prayer*. Translated by John Reumann. Philadelphia: Fortress, 1964.

———. *New Testament Theology*. Vol. 1. Translated by J. Bowden. London: Redwood, 1972.

———. *The Prayers of Jesus*. Translated by John Bowden et al. Philadelphia: Fortress, 1978.

———. "The Lord's Prayer in Matthew and Luke." In *The Lord's Prayer: Perspectives for Reclaiming Christian Prayer*, 56–70, edited by Daniel Migliore. Grand Rapids, Mich.: Eerdmans, 1993.

John Paul II. "Savifici doloris." 1981. http://www.vatican.va/content/john-paul-ii/en/apost_letters/1984/documents/hf_jp-ii_apl_11021984_salvifici-doloris.html.

Keener, Craig. *A Commentary on the Gospel of Matthew*. Grand Rapids, Mich.: Eerdmans, 1999.

Kistemaker, Simon. "The Lord's Prayer in the First Century." *Journal of Evangelical Theology Society* 21, no. 4 (1978): 323–28.

Knox, Ronald. *Pastoral and Occasional Sermons*. San Francisco: Ignatius Press, 2002.

Kwon, Junghoo. "Cyprian, Origen and the Lord's Prayer: Theological Diversities between Latin West and Greek East in the Third Century." *Asia Journal of Theology* 26, no. 1 (April 2012): 58–87.

Lampe, G. W. "'Our Father' in the Fathers." In *Christian Spirituality: Essays in Honour of Gordon Rupp*, 9–31, edited by Peter Brooks. London: S. C. M. Press, 1975.

Last, Hugh. "The Rotas-Sator Square: Present Positions and Future Prospects." *Journal of Theological Studies* 3, no. 1 (1952): 92–97.

Leibniz, Gottfried Wilhelm von. *Theodicy: Essays on the Goodness of God, the Freedom of Man, and the Origin of Evil*. Edited by Austin Farrer. Translated by E. M. Huggard. London: Routledge, 1952.

Léthel, F. M. *Théologie de l'agonie du Christ*. Paris: Éditions Beauchesne, 1996.

Lewis, C. S. *The Great Divorce*. New York: HarperCollins, 2001.

———. *The Discarded Image*. Cambridge: Cambridge University Press, 2013.

Lohfink, Gerhard. *Jesus of Nazareth: What He Wanted, Who He Was*. Collegeville, Minn.: Liturgical Press, 2012.

———. *The Our Father: A New Reading*. Collegeville, Minn.: Liturgical Press, 2019.

Lohmeyer, Ernst. *"Our Father": An Introduction to The Lord's Prayer*. Translated by J. Bowden. New York: Harper Collins, 1965.

Lombardo, Nicholas, OP. *The Father's Will: Christ's Crucifixion and the Goodness of God*. Oxford: Oxford University Press, 2013.

Luz, Ulrich. *Matthew 1–7: A Commentary*. Minneapolis: Fortress, 2007.

Maritain, Raïssa. *Notes on the Lord's Prayer*. Edited by Jacques Maritain. New York: P. J. Kennedy and Sons, 1963.

Marshall, I. H. *The Gospel of Luke*. Grand Rapids, Mich.: Eerdmans, 1978.

Mitch, Curtis, and Edward Sri. *The Gospel of Matthew*. Grand Rapids, Mich.: Baker Academic, 2010.

Morris, Michael. "Deuteronomy in the Matthean and Lucan Temptation in the Light of Early Jewish Antidemonic Tradition." *Catholic Biblical Quarterly* 78 (2016): 290–301.

Munari, Matteo. "Fa'che non cadiamo." In *Studium Biblicum Franciscanum: Liber Annus* LXIV, edited by L. Daniel Chrupcala, 165–82. Turnhout: Brepols, 2015.

Patrick, Dale. "The Kingdom of God in the Old Testament." In *The Kingdom of God in 20th-Century Interpretation*, edited by Wendell Willis, 67–79. Peabody, Mass.: Hendrickson, 1987.

Pennington, Jonathan. *Heaven and Earth in the Gospel of Matthew*. Ada, Mich.: Baker Academic, 2009.

Perl, Eric. *Theophany: The Neoplatonic Philosophy of Dionysius the Areopagite*. New York: State University of New York Press, 2007.

Pitre, Brant. *Jesus and the Last Supper*. Grand Rapids, Mich.: Eerdmans, 2015.

Plato. *Plato's "Parmenides": Translation and Analysis*. Translated by R. E. Allen. Minneapolis: University of Minnesota Press, 1983.

Pliny the Younger. *Letters: Books 1–7*. Edited and translated by Betty Radice. LCL vol. 55. Cambridge, Mass.: Harvard University Press, 1969.

Rordorf, Willy. "The Lord's Prayer in the Light of Its Liturgical Use in the Early Church." *Studia Liturgica* 14 (1980–81): 1–19.

Schnackenburg, Rudolf. *God's Rule and Kingdom*. New York: Herder and Herder, 1963.

Schürmann, Heinz. *Das Gebet des Herrn als Schlüssel zum Verstehen Jesu*. Leipzig: Herder, 1990.

Soulen, R. Kendall. "Hallowed Be Thy Name! The Tetragrammaton and the Name of the Trinity." In *Jews and Christians: People of God*, edited by Carl Braaten and Robert Jenson, 145–49. Grand Rapids: Eerdmans, 2003.

Stevenson, Kenneth. *The Lord's Prayer: A Text in Tradition*. Minneapolis: Fortress, 2004.

Vinel, Nicolas. "Le judaïsme caché du carré Sator de Pompéi." *Revue de l'histoire des religions* 223, no. 2 (2006): 173–194.

von Balthasar, Hans Urs. *Love Alone*. Translated by Alexander Dru. New York: Herder and Herder, 1969.

von Speyr, Adrienne. *Apokalypse: Betrachtungen über die Geheime Offenbarung*. Vienna: Verlag Herold, 1950.

Williamson, Peter. *Revelation*. Grand Rapids, Mich.: Baker Academic, 2015.

Wilken, Robert Louis. *The Spirit of Early Christian Thought: Seeking the Face of God*. New Haven: Yale University Press, 2003.

Wilkinson, Robert. *Tetragrammaton: Western Christians and the Hebrew Name of God*. Boston: Brill, 2015.

Wright, N. T. *Jesus and the Victory of God*: *Christian Origins and the Question of God*. Vol. 2. Minneapolis: Fortress, 1996.

———. *The Lord and His Prayer*. Grand Rapids, Mich.: Eerdmans, 1996.

Zaborowski, Holger. "'Hallowed Be Thy Name': Of God and Men and the Miracle of Language." *Communio* 43, no. 1 (2016): 7–15.

SCRIPTURE INDEX

GENERAL INDEX

adoption: divine, 18–31, 38–39, 42–43,
111, 137–38
Anderson, Gary, 111
angels, 10, 34, 38, 58, 76, 80, 84–87,
91–92. *See also isangelos*
aporia, 14–15
Ascension, 8, 22, 76–77
asceticism, xix, 39, 54, 71, 84–85, 100,
106, 131–32, 143–45, 147, 150,
152–54
Augustine of Hippo, xv, xx, 17–18, 22,
24, 28, 32, 33n2, 37, 39–40, 41n18,
46, 56n31, 77n37, 79, 87, 89n29,
102–3, 114, 115n19, 117, 137, 141, 149,
150

Balthasar, Hans Urs von, xiii, 57–58
baptism, 22–25, 27, 51, 54–55, 116, 120,
138, 143, 150
Basil of Caesarea, 142–43, 153, 155
Benedict XVI (pope), 60, 67–69
bread: material, 100–106; in New Testament, 97–99; in Old Testament,
96–97; spiritual, 101–3
Brown, Raymond E., xiv, 9

Celsus, 146, 155
Christ, xii, xix, xx, 4, 8–12, 16, 20–23,
25–30, 38, 40, 55–56, 58, 67–77, 81,
83, 89–91, 93, 101–7, 112, 115, 119, 121,
129, 136–37, 139. *See also* imitation;
Jesus
Chromatius of Aquileia, 25, 141, 150

Church, xi, xiii, xix, 7–9, 24, 27, 51, 57,
60, 68, 77, 89, 102–3, 105–6, 116, 131,
142, 146
Clement of Alexandria, 85, 151
concupiscence, 39–40
Constantinople, First Council, 143
covenant, 52, 61–62, 97, 113, 118, 120
creation, 9, 14, 20–21, 32, 34–38, 40, 43,
46, 49, 53, 55, 59, 64, 68–69, 72, 76,
79–80, 114, 126, 136
cross, the, 8–10, 15, 66, 76, 82–83, 91, 93,
103, 121, 136, 138–39
Culpepper, R. A., 111
Cyprian of Carthage, xv, xx, 23, 27, 39,
46, 55n27, 71, 88, 100, 102–3, 117,
133–34, 142, 151
Cyril of Jerusalem, xv, 25, 41n19, 105,
118, 142, 151

death, 10, 12, 22, 24, 64–65, 70, 76, 93,
117, 126, 128, 136, 139
debt: in the Fathers, 114–16; in Scriptures, 109–14
deification, 21, 25, 91, 93, 106
de Lubac, Henri, xiii, 17n2,
devil, 26, 50, 52, 69–70, 116, 122, 126–31,
133, 135, 137. *See also* Satan
Didache, 4–5, 7, 33, 140, 151
Dionysius the Areopagite, 18n4, 156

epiousios, 98–99, 101, 104–5
eschatology, 9, 62, 95, 112, 128. *See also*
salvation

Eucharist, 97–98, 102–6, 139, 142. *See also* liturgy

Evagrius of Pontus, 55, 72, 131–33, 136, 142, 152

evil, 9, 19, 25, 27, 83, 85–86, 95, 116, 122–23, 126, 130–40

Father: in the heavens, 32–33; the name, 16–31; unknowability, 17–18, 28

forgiveness: in the Fathers 114–21; in Scriptures, 109–14

France, R. T., 79

Francis (pope), 123

freedom, 10–11, 25, 30, 42, 54, 79, 90–93, 114, 130, 134. *See also* will

Gethsemane, 81, 83, 89–91, 139

grace, 4, 20, 22–23, 25–27, 29, 38, 43–44, 69, 74, 91–93, 106, 120, 132–33, 137, 140

Gregory of Nazianzus, 28–29, 142–43, 152, 155

Gregory of Nyssa, xv, xvii, 17, 19, 38n11, 41–42, 56, 71–72, 85n16, 87, 92, 109, 118–20, 136, 143, 152–53

Guardini, Romano, xiii, 8, 13

Gundry, R. H., 112

heaven: and earth, 34, 36, 80–81, 89–90; heavens, 33–34, 36; as place, 32–33, 35–36, 40–43

holiness, 46–48, 53, 56

Holy Spirit, xix, 23, 50–51, 72, 76–77, 115, 127

hope, 24, 39, 76–77, 93, 107, 112–14, 118, 135, 137, 139–40

image: of Christ, 25–26; of the Father, 26; of God, 40, 54, 56, 73, 77, 101, 120, 126

imitation: of God, 54–55, 58, 119–20; of Jesus, 54, 74, 80. *See also isangelos*

incarnation, 8, 11, 21–22, 24–25, 43, 90–91, 121

Irenaeus of Lyon, 11n14

isangelos, 39–40, 84–87

Israel, 46–49, 60–62, 64–66, 97, 113, 118, 124, 134

Jerome of Stridon, xx, 54, 74, 104–5, 141, 143, 153–54

Jesus: agony and the cup, 89–90. *See also* Ascension; Christ; cross; incarnation; will

John Cassian, 23, 42, 52, 55, 70, 86, 105, 144, 154

John Chrysostom, 24, 42–43, 53, 75, 87, 116–18, 130, 141, 144, 147, 154

John Paul II (pope), 137

jubilee, 113–14, 121

judgment, 62, 74, 77, 112, 117–18, 121, 129. *See also* eschatology

kingdom: in biblical studies, 60; in the Fathers, 69–78; in New Testament, 63–69; in Old Testament, 60–63

Knox, Ronald, 29–30

Leibnitz, Gottfried Wilhelm, 78

Lewis, C. S., 32

Libanius, 144

likeness: angelic, 85; divine, 19, 25, 27, 73–74, 88, 92, 101, 118–20

liturgy, 4, 6–7, 58, 69, 103, 142. *See also* Eucharist

logismos, 131–32

Lohfink, Gerhard, 60, 65–67, 73n28

Lord's Prayer: petitions, 13; versions, 4–6

Luz, Ulrich, 79, 99

Macarius of Egypt, 85n16, 154

Maritain, Raïssa, 13

Master, the, 30, 89, 121, 136, 140, 145, 154

Maximus the Confessor, xx, 18, 21–22, 26, 39, 40n17, 52, 54n26, 72–74, 86, 90–91, 94, 100, 114, 120, 130, 135, 145, 155

monophysitism, 146
monothelitism, 90–91, 145

name: of the Father, 17–19, 26, 33; of
    God, 36, 45–52, 54, 57; of Jesus,
    50–55; significance in antiquity,
    46–47, 51–52
neo-Platonism, 156
Nicaea, First Council, 142

obedience: of angels, 86; of humans,
    21n7, 83, 87, 91, 93, 112, 139; of Jesus,
    80–86, 89–91, 93
Origen of Alexandria, xx, 5–6, 14, 26,
    31, 33, 37–38, 41–42, 51–53, 70, 73,
    85n14, 90, 98–99, 101, 104–5, 115,
    122, 133–35, 146, 155

Paradise, 40–42, 62
Paul (apostle), 20, 30, 51–52, 82–83,
    119, 129
peirasmos, 122; as temptation, 126–28;
    as trial or test, 123–25
penance, 132
Perl, Eric, 136
Peter Chrysologus, xv, 21–22, 24–26,
    37, 52, 54–55, 70, 75, 84, 103, 118, 135,
    146, 156
philanthropia, 53, 97, 115
pilgrimage, xix, 36, 40–44, 75, 106, 128,
    138, 140
Pliny the Elder, 1
Pliny the Younger, 1
prayer, xix. See also Lord's Prayer
Proba, Anicia Faltonia, 141, 149
prodigal son, 41–42

Ratzinger, Joseph, xiii. See also Bene-
    dict XVI
reason, 40, 100
ressourcement, xi–xiii
Resurrection, 22, 38, 71–72, 76, 82,
    84, 96
ROTAS-SATOR square, 2–4, 8–9, 128

salvation, xiii, 52, 61, 66, 81, 95, 103, 106,
    116, 121
Satan, 70, 76–77, 126–27
Scriptures: and the Fathers, xiii–xiv,
    xix, 14; and ressourcement, xiv; and
    versions of the Lord's Prayer, 4–6,
    12. See also aporia
Septuagint, 49
Sermon on the Mount, 5–6
sin, 5–6, 11, 19, 26, 28, 30, 38n11, 42–43,
    51, 53–55, 64, 69–70, 72, 74, 76–78,
    83–84, 87–88, 97, 103, 109–20,
    122–28, 130–36, 139

temptation. See peirasmos
Tertullian, xiv, 8, 59, 88, 90, 100, 102,
    122, 147, 151, 156
tetragrammaton, 47–50
theodicy, 78, 93, 136
Theodore of Mopsuestia, 22–24, 28, 38,
    54, 70–71, 89, 130, 147, 154
thought. See logismos
transcendence: divine, 17, 34–37, 43, 53
trial. See peirasmos
Trinity, 18n3, 21, 29, 38, 50, 71, 72n25,
    76, 115, 143, 150, 152, 154

Vatican, Second Council, xi, xiii, 11
vice, 26, 28, 39, 54, 58, 70, 152
virtue, 10, 25–26, 29, 39, 54, 56, 70,
    72–74, 119, 123, 134, 153–54
von Speyr, Adrienne, 11

Wilken, Robert Louis, xix, 91
will: of angels, 92; of the Father, 81–82,
    93; of God, 79–80; of humans, 80,
    87–89, 92, 135, 139; of Jesus, 81–82,
    90–91, 139. See also obedience
wisdom, 101, 104–6
Word (Logos): Scriptures, xiii–xix, 14,
    38, 102, 106; the Son, 8, 10–11, 26,
    40, 68, 76, 92, 100–101, 104
Wright, N. T., 60, 63–65

Mysteries of the Lord's Prayer: Wisdom from the Early Church was designed in Garamond with Mr Eaves display type and composed by Kachergis Book Design of Pittsboro, North Carolina. It was printed on 60-pound Natural Eggshell and bound by McNaughton & Gunn of Saline, Michigan.